Embassy of Onesimus

THE LETTER OF PAUL TO PHILEMON

Allen Dwight Callahan

THE NEW TESTAMENT IN CONTEXT

Howard Clark Kee and J. Andrew Overman, editors

TRINITY PRESS INTERNATIONAL

Valley Forge, Pennsylvania

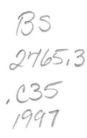

BS
2765.3
.C35
1997

Trinity Press International
P.O. Box 851, Valley Forge, PA 19482–0851

Trinity Press International is a division of
the Morehouse Publishing Group

Library of Congress Cataloging-in-Publication Data

Callahan, Allen Dwight.
    Embassy of Onesimus : the letter of Paul to Philemon / by Allen
Dwight Callahan.
       p. cm. – (The New Testament in context)
    Includes bibliographical references and index.
    ISBN 1-56338-147-8 (pbk. : alk. paper)
    1. Bible. N.T. Philemon – Commentaries. I. Title. II. Series.
BS2765.3.C35 1997
227'.86077 – dc21
                                                        97-214
                                                          CIP

Printed in the United States of America

97 98 99 00 01   10 9 8 7 6 5 4 3 2 1

To my grandfather, John T. Savage (1911–1995),
beloved husband, father, and faithful member
of Allen AME Church in Philadelphia

Contents

Preface

I offer this essay to make history: to make history of interpretation, of pastoral theology, of New Testament ethics. I essay to do so by rereading a piece of the apostle Paul's correspondence that already has a long history of having been read many times by many audiences. Most of those audiences were not the letter's intended addressees but earnest, theologically interested voyeurs. Paul's correspondence is fraught with conflict and controversy that still today makes his letters a fascinating afterimage of a complicated multiparty conversation. Headaches and heartaches make for fascinating reading, especially if they are not one's own.

But some would argue that the thrill is gone. Paul's letters have been an obsessive focus of luxuriant theological attention at least since the Reformation. Especially hackneyed is the commentary on Paul's short epistle to Philemon and two of his colleagues, presumably leaders of a Christian house assembly in an undisclosed location. All modern commentaries essentially agree with an interpretation bequeathed to us from late antiquity that the letter treats the case of Onesimus, a pilfering runaway slave, whom Paul is attempting to rehabilitate in the eyes of Philemon, his rightfully angry master. This story has been told and retold, in countless commentaries and sermons, and so it appears there is little to add to the interpretation of this brief and thoroughly exegeted epistle.

In this commentary, however, I tell another story: a story of the estrangement of two Christian brothers, Onesimus and Philemon. This reading of the rhetorical situation and reconstruction of the historical situation provides a new narrative for the letter. The interpretation for which I argue in the following pages is one that I found I share, much to my own surprise, with several nineteenth-century American abolitionist interpreters. The introduction and commentary that follow here are expansions of and, I hope, improvements upon arguments I have put forward in two articles published in the *Harvard Theological Review*.* Those who are familiar with these articles may recognize much of the thinking and some of the prose here. In addition I have sought not only to expand and improve my alternative reading but to advance it as well by exploring the letter's contemporary significance. Having said something about what the letter meant, or at least could have meant, to its first audiences, I then say something about what it means, or at least could mean, now. I argue that this alternative reading of the letter offers a paradigm for Christian reconciliation that includes diplomacy, persuasion, forbearance, and reparations for injured parties. In other words, the letter speaks of the challenging implications of Christian love and the imperative of Christian justice. If there is an interpretation of great moment to be offered for this otherwise unremarkable piece of correspondence, then the treatment of these themes holds the promise of such an interpretation.

It is neither practicable nor desirable for me to survey comprehensively a tradition of interpretation that is both rich and redundant. I have limited myself, therefore, to the representative and the idiosyncratic. With only occasional sidelong glances at other exegetes, I have chosen to carry on my argument with the reigning interpretation by interrogating John Chrysostom, Martin Luther, and J. B. Lightfoot, voices from patristic antiquity, the late Middle Ages, and industrial modernity, respectively. Each is a towering exegete of enduring influence. All others stand upon their shoulders or in their shadow; with erudition and eloquence these strong voices say what other commentators have but echoed. I also treat the traditional interpretation as a whole in the introduction of this work; this is my attempt to provide

---

*"Paul's Epistle to Philemon: Toward an Alternative *Argumentum*," *Harvard Theological Review* 86, no. 4 (1993): 357–76; "John Chrysostom on Philemon: A Response to Margaret M. Mitchell" *Harvard Theological Review* 88, no. 1 (1995): 149–56.

a genealogy for a reading almost sixteen centuries old. Having surveyed the field in the introduction, I then put my exegetical hand to the plow in the commentary. Much commentary that is based upon traditional interpretation and is obviously contrary to my own reconstruction of the letter's situation in life I have simply left behind in silence, without looking back. I have tried to reproduce here in full for the reader's convenience some of the texts to which I refer that may not be readily available or well known, and when published translations have not been available or helpful I have provided my own. I have also included the Greek words and text where it is important and where immediate reference to the original language may be helpful, but otherwise I supply translations and transliterations.

On the one hand, the text of Paul's epistle to Philemon barely takes up one full printed page: even scholarly perversity and the academic obsession with minutiae cannot extrude lengthy commentary from so little textual raw material. On the other hand, much could have been included that I have left out. But I have exercised restraint in an effort to be clear, concise, and simple, but not too simple. I leave the evaluation of success in this and all other efforts here, of course, to the reader.

Acknowledgments

I am indebted to the following people for their contributions to this work. First, many thanks to Helmut Koester, teacher, colleague, and friend, for his encouragement and counsel at every stage of this project. He may still disagree fundamentally with many of the things I say here, but he has repeatedly defended my right to say them. In so doing, he has exemplified and continues to model the generosity and broadmindedness of scholarship at its best, a spirit of open discourse that is also very American, his persistent German accent notwithstanding. Thanks also to Tamar Duke Cohen at the *Harvard Theological Review* for permission to borrow freely from the two articles on Philemon I published in *HTR,* both of which benefited enormously from the characteristically careful and thoughtful attentions of the *HTR* editorial staff. Many thanks to Professor Obery Hendricks of Drew University Divinity School, who encouraged me to engage what is interesting, important, and thus controversial in the pages to follow. Thanks also to Missy Daniel, editor of the *Harvard Divinity Bulletin,* for her critical reading of the entire manuscript of this work: her comments and criticisms have saved me from much infelicity, inaccuracy, and inscrutability. I have already thanked Professor Margaret Mitchell in print for her critical review of my arguments in her *HTR* article:* my thinking, and thus this work as a whole, are better for her thoughtful engagement. In the academy, it is engagement, not agreement, that advances our understanding, and my own understanding of

---

*Margaret M. Mitchell, "John Chrysostom on Philemon: A Second Look" *Harvard Theological Review* 88, no. 1 (1995): 135–48.

Philemon has been so advanced, though Professor Mitchell and others may not think so on the basis of what I have written here. And special thanks to my publisher, Hal Rast, and his associates at Trinity Press International for their diligence, forbearance, and kind attention in bringing this work to press.

Finally, I offer humble thanks to my American ancestors: though so grievously wronged, they were right to question the apostolic sanction of their chains. If this work affords some small vindication of their insights, then my labor shall not have been in vain.

Introduction

With their own indigenous hermeneutic of suspicion, African American slaves questioned both the authorship and theological import of Paul's epistle to Philemon. The Rev. J. Colcock Jones, a white Methodist missionary to slaves in Georgia in the second quarter of the nineteenth century, filed this report to his mission board recounting the response of slaves to a sermon for which the epistle to Philemon was the text.

> I was preaching to a large congregation on the Epistle to Philemon: and when I insisted on fidelity and obedience as Christian virtues in servants, and upon the authority of Paul, condemned the practice of running away, one-half of my audience deliberately rose up and walked off with themselves; and those who remained looked anything but satisfied with the preacher or his doctrine. After dismission, there was no small stir among them; some solemnly declared that there was no such Epistle in the Bible; others, that it was not the Gospel; others, that I preached to please the masters; others, that they did not care if they never heard me preach again.[1]

The slaves themselves brought a radical critique to the purported apostolic sanction of slavery. Some apparently never believed it; that is, they never believed the traditional interpretation, which may be summarized as follows: "The Letter to Philemon, a resident of Colossae in Phrygia, is a model of Christian tactfulness in seeking to effect reconciliation between Onesimus, the runaway slave, and his master, who according to Roman law had absolute authority over the person and life of his slave."[2]

1

And I never really believed it myself. I never believed the traditional interpretation. Perhaps I never believed it because, as an impressionable young student of the Bible, I had never heard it. My first encounter with Holy Writ was the review of Bible stories in the Sunday school lessons of the local church I attended as a child. The story of Adam and Eve. The story of Abraham and Sarah. The story of David and Goliath. The stories of Solomon and Bathsheba, Elijah and Elisha, Jesus and Mary, Peter and John, Paul and Silas. The story of Onesimus and Philemon, the "once-upon-a-time-there-was-a-slave-named-Onesimus" story, was not among them: there was no such epistle in the Bible, as far as I knew at the time. The Sunday school class I attended was one of the dozen or so that met before morning worship at Allen African Methodist Episcopal Church in Philadelphia, the birthplace of the African Methodist Episcopal denomination. Allen AME Church was named after Richard Allen, founder and first bishop of the denomination. In 1799 Allen and several other African Americans walked off with themselves in protest of the racially discriminatory practices of the Methodist Episcopal Church, a British religious import that was quickly acclimating itself to colonial North American racism. Later in his life, Allen recounted in a memoir the signal incident of his defection:

> A number of us usually attended St. George's church in Fourth street; and when the colored people began to get numerous in attending the church, they moved us from the seats we usually sat on, and placed us around the wall, and on Sabbath morning we went to church and the sexton stood at the door, and told us to go in the gallery. He told us to go, and we would see where to sit. We expected to take seats over the ones we formerly occupied below, not knowing any better. We took those seats. Meeting had begun, and they were nearly done singing, and just as we got to the seats, the elder said, "Let us pray." We had not been long on our knees before I heard considerable scuffling and low talking. I raised my head up and saw one of the trustees, H—— M——, having hold of Rev. Absalom

Jones, pulling him up off of his knees, and saying, "You must get up —you must not kneel here." Mr. Jones replied, "Wait until prayer is over." Mr. H—— M—— said, "No, you must get up now, or I will call for aid and force you away." Mr. Jones said, "Wait until prayer is over, and I will get up and trouble you no more." With that he beckoned to one of the other trustees, Mr. L—— S—— to come to his assistance. He came, and went to William White to pull him up. By this time prayer was over, and we all went out of the church in a body, and they were no more plagued with us in the church.[3]

I was spiritual heir to these ecclesiastical wildcat strikers. Determined to preserve their Christian liberty, they proved too restive for any existing denomination, and so founded their own; it was the first Christian denomination founded in the United States. Richard Allen and his associates walked off with themselves, out of a humiliating second-class citizenship and into American religious history. They walked off with themselves into incipient pan-Africanism, for they were to call their new denomination the African Methodist Episcopal Church. They understood themselves to be daughters and sons of Africa, though born and raised, rooted and grounded in the young United States. This qualified pan-Africanism caused Allen and his co-religionists to claim stubbornly their African ancestry and at the same time to resist and condemn attempts by American politicians to repatriate African Americans in Africa as a solution to what would someday come to be called "the Negro Question." They also walked off with themselves into incipient black nationalism, a racially chauvinistic brand of radicalism that was self-consciously Christian, that was not secularized until the middle of the twentieth century. AME Bishop Henry McNeal Turner, a century after Allen's permanent departure from Methodist apartheid, demanded that all images of the blond-haired, blue-eyed Jesus be removed from African American churches and replaced with images that depicted the son of God as a black man. African American Christianity continues to offer up robust forms of black nationalism even in our own time, its fruit never having fallen far from the tree of Allen's pro-African separatism. Though this radicalism has all but disappeared in the AME Church itself, its spirit continues to animate the efforts of some contemporary African American churchmen and churchwomen who have consciously and unconsciously emulated Allen's praxis of protest, secession, and independence.

These peculiar Christians insisted on following the directive of the Negro spiritual, "Walk together, children / Don't you get weary." They walked together in an ecclesiastical union, they walked off with themselves. Refusing to get weary, they never stopped walking. They would not sit for disenfranchisement, indignity, and servility. And they would not stand for a pro-slavery Paul. So I never heard the epistle to Philemon preached or taught in my home church. My forebears had declared a perpetual wildcat strike against such ideology over a century and a half before my first Sunday school class at Allen AME Church.

•

I learned later, in the academy, of Paul's purported complicity with slave regimes ancient and modern. A solid consensus of learned exegetes represented by John Chrysostom in late antiquity, Martin Luther at the end of the Middle Ages, and Bishop Lightfoot at the zenith of industrial strength modernity had read the epistle as a letter of introduction for a slave who was both a criminal and a fugitive. With modernity, however, commentators intensified the association of the epistle with slavery, and in discussions of slavery and the Bible the letter was offered as an important exhibit in arguing any case for Paul's position on the peculiar institution. In 1964, the international index of contemporary biblical scholarship *Elenchus Bibliographicus Biblicus,* having listed together up to that time works treating Colossians and Philemon, provided Colossians with its own heading and introduced a new rubric: "Philemon; Slavery in the NT." The publication apparatus of the academy had institutionalized the conventional wisdom about this epistle: Philemon and ancient slavery were inextricably tied to one another.

So firmly established is the interpretation of the epistle as a "cover letter" for a repentant runaway slave addressed to his irritated master, that any discussion of slavery in the New Testament invariably alludes to Paul's epistle to Philemon; all recent commentators on the epistle include in their respective treatments a disquisition on ancient slavery.[4] Even in his methodologically sophisticated study of the "narrative world" of Philemon, Norman Petersen begins his summary of the "story" behind the letter as follows: "Once upon a time there was a runaway slave named Onesimus...."[5] He construed the epistle as a delicate and canny intervention on the part of the Apostle into the problematic of Christian relations under the Roman slave regime, this in spite of the concession on the part of modern exegetes that Philemon fails to elucidate Paul's attitudes either toward slaves in particular or the institution of slavery in general.[6] Reference to Philemon in discussions of slavery have frequently proved inconclusive, yet scholarship is now so constrained by centuries of exegetical tradition that it is impossible to talk about the epistle without talking about ancient slavery and vice versa.

But in the beginning it was not so.

The commentaries claim that Onesimus is a fugitive, yet there are no verbs of flight in the entire epistle. Nor is any reason offered in the text for his flight. R. Lehmann comments, "It is difficult to know why [Onesimus ran away]. Was his master severe? It does not seem so. Philemon appears throughout the letter as a good and generous man."[7] Lehmann here betrays a scholarly naiveté regarding the unsavory realities of Roman slavery. Cruelty of a master toward his slave can never be ruled out in the Graeco-Roman world, where severity bordering on sadism was a common feature of the servile relationship.[8] Mildness and forbearance in this respect would have made Philemon not only an exception but an oddity in his own world, so conditioned by violence against all purported inferiors.[9]

Here Lehmann has highlighted a problem not solved but created by the prevailing exegesis. Nowhere is it explicitly stated that Onesimus had run away, and the motive for such action is equally obscure. The entire fugitive slave hypothesis was cogently challenged by John Knox,[10] but unfortunately his well-reasoned objections were lost in his collapsing theory regarding the origin and relation of Philemon and Colossians.[11] Arguments for the untenability of the fugitive slave hypothesis have been recovered from the rubble only recently and augmented in the independent treatments of Peter Lampe[12] and Sarah Winter.[13] Lampe argues that according to the authoritative opinions of several Roman jurists, if, indeed, Onesimus came to Paul for intercession, such a situation does not constitute flight. The jurists opine explicitly that a slave seeking out a friend of his master to serve as intercessor is not to be considered a fugitive.[14] Lampe also finds it inconceivable that Paul would express no concern about the brutal punishment prescribed by Roman law and custom that awaited Onesimus had he been guilty of running away.[15] Winter's more extensive treatment cites not only the silence of the text but its structure as well. She notes that the thanksgiving section at the beginning of the letter makes no mention of the circumstances surrounding Onesimus's arrival; yet Paul Schubert's study of the introductory thanksgiving section of Paul's letters has demonstrated that the thanksgiving sets the epistolary situation: it informs the recipient of important events that have taken place since the last communication and introduces the theme of the letter. Paul's failure to recount the conditions of Onesimus's arrival, Winter argues, therefore indicates that the recipient, i.e., Philemon, already knew that Onesimus was with Paul.[16]

Parallels from other ancient letters have been offered in support of the fugitive slave hypothesis, but on close examination this evidence is also less than compelling. Eduard Lohse cites the letter of a fourth-century Christian priest in Hermoupolis to a Christian officer in the Fayûm on behalf of a soldier named Paul who had deserted his post:

> To my master and beloved brother Abinneus the Praepositus — Caor, Papas of Hermoupolis, greeting. I salute your children much. I would have you know, lord, about Paul the soldier, concerning his flight. Pardon him this once, seeing that I am without leisure to come to you at this

present. And, if he desist not, he will come again into your hands another time. Be well, I pray, many years, my lord brother.[17]

The priest writes to the officer, "...about Paul...concerning his flight, pardon him...," elements we would expect to see in the Apostle's epistle to Philemon to corroborate the fugitive slave hypothesis. The absence of these elements, in contrast to the letter from Hermoupolis, is conspicuous. The celebrated intercessory letter of Pliny the Younger to Sabinianus (*Ep.* 9.21), first suggested as a parallel to Philemon at the end of the sixteenth century by Joachim Camerarius[18] and adduced in 1642 by Hugo Grotius in his *Annotationes in Epistolem ad Philemonem*,[19] on closer inspection is even more disappointing.

To Sabinianus. Your freedman, whom you lately mentioned as having displeased you, came to me and threw himself at my feet as much as he would have done at yours. He has wept a lot, he has pled a lot, and he has even been silent a lot; he has done all these things to convince me of his penitence. I really believe he has reformed, because he has a sense of his delinquency. I know you are angry, and I know that you are angry with good reason. But forbearance is all the more praiseworthy when the cause of anger is quite justified. You have loved the man and, I hope, you shall love him; in the meantime, let me only encourage you to pardon him. Should he anger you hereafter, you will have so much the stronger plea in excuse for your anger if you show yourself more indulgent to him now. Make some allowance for his youth, his tears, and your own indulgence. Neither torture him nor torture yourself; for a man of your benevolence of heart cannot be angry without upsetting himself. I am afraid I may seem not to request but compel you to forgive him if I add my pleas to his. Nevertheless I will; and so much more fully and freely since I sharply and severely reproved him, having threatened to never again plead for him after this. That was for him, because he ought to be frightened; for you it is not the same thing. I may, perhaps,

again so plead, and again obtain your forgiveness. It may be
such for me to plead, and for you to forgive. Farewell.[20]

Pliny's letter is on behalf of a nameless *libertus*, "freedman,"
not a *servus*, "slave," and the two letters are worlds apart in style.
F. Forrester Church, in his analysis of the rhetorical structure
of Philemon, notes that "in deliberative rhetoric, success rests
on establishing two primary motives for action, honor (*honestas*)
and advantage (*utilitas*)."[21] This is a perfect description of Pliny's
appeal, but it has no point of contact with Paul's. As Knox has
observed,

> Pliny says exactly what we should expect such a note to say.
> Paul, on the other hand, does not say some of the things
> we should expect him to say and says others which seem
> scarcely relevant.... Paul says not one word about any re-
> pentance on the part of the slave and there is no explicit
> appeal for forgiveness or pity on the part of the master. In
> other words, the terms we should expect such a letter to
> contain in abundance are simply not there at all. *This fact
> alone should lead us to suspect a rather deeper purpose in the
> letter than the obvious one generally assigned.*[22]

Pliny's letter to Sabinianus thus offers a poor parallel for what we
find in Paul's epistle. In fact, we have no letters of intercession
on behalf of a runaway slave that may be compared to Philemon, and scholars consequently have grasped at straws to argue
for the relevance of purported parallels. In an attempt to defend the fugitive slave hypothesis, John G. Nordling marshals
as epistolary parallels three papyrus letters treating of runaway
slaves. Though conceding to Knox's criticism that Pliny's letter
is essentially dissimilar to Philemon,[23] Nordling himself admits
that the papyri are "not as immediately applicable to Philemon
as Pliny."[24] Nordling in effect has offered new evidence of even
more dubious relevance than the old, and this by his own admission. All the above-mentioned parallels contribute little to a
critically defensible interpretation of Philemon.

A disturbing corollary of the fugitive slave hypothesis is the
proposition that Onesimus was seeking to escape punishment

for a crime he had committed. Lehmann asks, "Had Onesimus seriously deceived his master, having committed a theft?"[25] J. B. Lightfoot is more forthright.

> He [i.e., Onesimus] was a thief and a runaway. His offence did not differ in any way, so far as we know, from the vulgar type of slavish offences. He seems to have done just what the representative slave in the Roman comedy threatens to do, when he gets into trouble. He had "packed up some goods and taken to his heels." Rome was the natural cesspool for these offscourings of humanity. In the thronging crowds of the metropolis was his best hope of secrecy. In the dregs of the city rabble he would find the society of congenial spirits.[26]

Such speculation is indefensible for reasons beyond its lack of foundation in the text. We know that masters were commonly cruel enough to put their slaves to flight.[27] But more importantly, this kind of uncharitable guesswork buys into the stereotype of the thieving, indolent slave that is part of the mythology of all slaveholding societies. This stereotype, be it of the "little Greek," or *graeculus,* of the Principate or the "Sambo" of the antebellum North American slavocracy,[28] is, as Harvard sociologist Orlando Patterson has observed, "an ideological imperative of all systems of slavery.... It is simply an elaboration of the notion that the slave is quintessentially a person without honor."[29] Stanley Elkins summarizes the stereotype: "docile but irresponsible, loyal but lazy, humble but chronically given to lying and stealing."[30] That the slaves of Roman comedy and satire fit this description tells us only that the comedians and the satirists, themselves mouthpieces of the ruling class, present us not with historical facts but mythological fabrications projected out of their own class hostility, embellished though they be with realities of slavery and domination. These fabrications comprise the literary image of the slave, in Lightfoot's words, "so far as we know." It is incumbent upon historians to discern the difference between mythology and history as keenly here as elsewhere.

Though interpreters have claimed that Onesimus is the slave of Philemon, in no place are the two names conjoined in any possessive construction, nor is Philemon referred to anywhere as *kurios,* "lord," or *despotēs,* "master," Lightfoot[31] and others since have put forward literary and inscriptional evidence indicating that the name "Onesimus" was borne by those either of servile status or background. But this association has been refuted by G. H. R. Horsley's examination of newly discovered inscriptions from the Roman imperial period. On the basis of these inscriptions he concludes: "These examples show that the name Onesimos could be borne by free persons of no insignificant status and that it is far from being a sure indication of servile status."[32]

The weight of establishing Onesimus's servile identity thus falls to verse 16a, "...receive him no longer as a slave, but more than a slave." All considerations of slavery rest on this one clause. The key word in this verse, however, is not "slave," *doulon,* but "as," *hōs,* in that it indicates a virtual, not an actual state of affairs. In the verse immediately following (17b), Paul exhorts Philemon to receive Onesimus *hōs eme,* "as (you would) me." Onesimus is to be received as Paul's virtual presence; he is not Paul, of course, but is to be treated as if he were Paul. Likewise, in verse 16a *hōs* indicates that Paul is speaking not of Onesimus's actual status, but of Philemon's attitude toward Onesimus and thus Onesimus's virtual status in Philemon's eyes. Nothing in the text conclusively indicates that Onesimus was ever the chattel of the letter's chief addressee, and the expectations fostered by the traditional fugitive slave hypothesis go unrealized in the letter. Modern commentators, even those most firmly committed to the prevailing interpretation, have tacitly admitted as much.

Furthermore, in the effective history of the text this hypothesis has been controverted. Antebellum abolitionists forwarding biblical arguments in the first half of the nineteenth century made observations much like those above about the dearth of evidence for the traditional interpretation of the epistle, and their objections to the slave hypothesis have yet to be adequately answered. In antebellum exegesis, the text of Philemon was a favored terrain of ideological contestation in controversialist slavery literature. Garry Wills has observed that "this genuine letter of Paul [i.e., Philemon] was not a favorite with American slaveholders,"[33] but this is only true for the letter as interpreted in abolitionist propaganda. Pro-slavery advocates, who referred to the epistle as "the Pauline Mandate,"[34] cited Philemon in support of both the institution of slavery and the dreaded Fugitive Slave Law, which required slaves in flight to be returned to their masters under penalty of law even when apprehended in free states.[35] Anti-slavery exegetes put to proof both the epistle and its traditional interpretation. Nineteenth-century abolitionist exegesis suggested an alternative hypothesis for the letter's life situation. In a pamphlet entitled *A Condensed Anti-Slavery Bible Argument,* Virginian George Bourne examines the epistle to Philemon in continuation of his critique of "Pro-Slavery Perversions of the New Testament."

> A slight examination of the epistle assures us that Philemon was a member of the Christian church, but there is not a particle of evidence in it to prove that he was a slaveholder, but the reverse.... Nor is there any evidence that Onesimus was a slave, but the reverse. The too-common pro-slavery assumption that they respectively were such, is therefore a mere begging of the question; and that not only without, but against the evidence furnished by the same epistle.[36]

Three years after Bourne, John Gregg Fee offered a similar interpretation in his pamphlet of abolitionist biblical arguments. Based on a careful review of the language of v. 16, Fee also suggested that Philemon and Onesimus were really brothers:

> There is evidence in the epistle that Onesimus was a natural brother to Philemon.... Paul calls him "a brother beloved, especially to me, but how much more unto thee both IN THE FLESH and in the Lord...." To Paul, Onesimus was a brother, especially or peculiarly beloved in the Lord, — as a christian, — in a spiritual sense. To Philemon he was not only a brother specially beloved in the Lord, but also a brother specially beloved in the flesh. (And Paul knew from a previous acquaintance, this attachment and blood relationship.)[37]

These responses of antebellum American interpreters show that the prevailing interpretation of Philemon is far from self-evident and beyond dispute in American biblical criticism; the religion of pro-slavery apologists had its cultured and not so cultured despisers who on reasoned grounds called into question the traditional pro-slavery interpretation.

●

There is little internal evidence to substantiate the hypothesis that Philemon is a letter of reintroduction for a repentant runaway slave. Nor does the ubiquity of this interpretation in medieval and modern treatments in and of itself legitimate this hypothesis as a valid historical reconstruction of the epistle's life situation. The kind of early testimony that would inform such a reconstruction is indeed sparse. The only sure ante-Nicene witness to Philemon is Tertullian who, while questioning Marcion's inconsistency in retaining Philemon in his canon while rejecting 1 and 2 Timothy and Titus, offers no comment on the contents of the letter itself (*Adversus Marcionem* 5.21). Regrettably, only a fragment of Rufinus's Latin translation of Origen's commentary on Philemon is extant, in which Origen, recounting the faith of the patriarchs, prophets, Jesus, and the Twelve, says nothing about Philemon or Onesimus.[38]

Until the fifth century the Syrian church rejected Philemon as spurious, preferring instead the more theologically substantial 3 Corinthians.[39] On this point the Syrians anticipated objections voiced in the middle of the nineteenth century by F. C. Baur, who dismissed Philemon as a pseudepigraphical "Christian romance,"[40] and by the incredulous African American slaves of Rev. Jones's congregation mentioned above. Perhaps Jerome had the Syrians in mind when he remarked in the preface to his commentary on Philemon, "In this way these and others determine that the epistle which was written to Philemon was not Paul's, or, if it was Paul's, that it has nothing that could edify us."[41] Theodore of Mopsuestia had to begin his own comments on the epistle with the acknowledgment that many regarded it as insignificant.[42]

Up to the end of the fourth century of the Common Era, Christendom was notably unimpressed by the epistle. As Lightfoot noted more than a century ago, "In the fourth century there was a strong bias against [Philemon].... We may infer from the replies of Jerome, of Chrysostom, and Theodore of Mopsuestia, that they felt themselves to be stemming a fierce current of prejudice which had set in this direction."[43] Handley C. G. Moule conjectured that the superscript to Philemon found in a tenth-century Greek manuscript, which reads, "Paul writes these sure (*bebaia*) words as a letter to faithful Philemon," has been emended by a reverent copyist, and that the original superscript read, in perfect hexameter verse, "Paul on a trifling (*baia*) theme thus writes to the faithful Philemon." The proposed emendation was made by changing the word *baia*, "trifling," to *bebaia*, "sure, established," thus returning a favorable judgment on the epistle but ruining the meter of the superscript:[44] a conjectural emendation which, like Voltaire's God, would have to have been invented if it didn't already exist, given the disaffection of the epistle's ancient audience.

It is in the face of this apparent disaffection that John Chrysostom wrote his remarks at the end of the fourth century. Chrysostom stridently insists on the epistle's importance: "But then some say that this epistle is superfluous and to be laid aside; if indeed it is concerned with a trifling matter, with one man, let them learn, as many as level these charges, that they are worthy of many charges...."[45] It is in Chrysostom's *hypothesis* or argument prefacing his first homily on Philemon that the now-traditional reconstruction of the epistle's life situation first appears.[46] "First it is necessary," writes Chrysostom, "to state the argument of the epistle, then also the matters that are questioned respecting it. What is the argument?" He then proposes that Onesimus is a fugitive slave on whose behalf Paul writes to Philemon, a proposition which he introduces with the words, "Therefore it seems to me...."[47] The diction of Chrysostom's argument indicates that he is offering the rationale for an opinion. Nothing in his words suggests that Chrysostom is drawing on an interpretation either current or traditional. Precisely the contrary: in his *hypothesis* Chrysostom is offering a novel interpretation and is thus constrained to argue for its validity. If any position may be understood as *au courant,* it is that of the unimpressed. A British patristics scholar acknowledged as much over a century ago: Chrysostom "is at pains to shew [sic] how the Epistle is of varied practical importance."[48] So Chrysostom begins his defense of the epistle with the words "some say," *tines phasi.* Chrysostom is citing here a traditional allegation against the epistle, which may have been before him in writing.[49]

Chrysostom, therefore, must be seen as challenging the prevailing negative assessment of Philemon by providing an innovative interpretation for the letter. From Paul's epistle to Philemon, shortest of the *corpus Paulinum,*[50] Chrysostom is able to derive an exegesis treating an issue of great moment in his own time — slavery. Apparently the reputed position of some in the Christian community on this important issue was a little too radical for Chrysostom's comfort. In his *argumentum* for Philemon, Chrysostom comes down hard on the side of law and order, anxious to dispel the disestablishmentarian reputation of the Christianity of his day with respect to slaves.

> But what is more important than all, that the word of God be not blasphemed, as he [i.e., Paul] himself says in one of his Epistles. "Let as many servants as are under the yoke count their own masters worthy of all honor, that the name of God and his doctrine be not blasphemed" (1 Tim. 6:1). For the Gentiles also will say, that even one who is a slave can be well pleasing to God. But now many are reduced to the necessity of blasphemy, and of saying Christianity has been introduced into life for the subversion of everything, masters having their servants taken from them, and it is a matter of violence.[51]

Chrysostom's claim of "subversion," even if hyperbolic, is remarkable. Apparently a Christian anti-slavery wing was wresting slaves away from their masters. (Exactly by what means we cannot be sure: were the efforts of these Christian abolitionists literally "a matter of violence"?) The reputation of the Christian community was being ruined by libertarian extremists who had disregarded the Pauline exhortation to servile obedience. These nameless Christians were challenging the Roman slavocracy, the constitutive element of a tottering late imperial hegemony. Chrysostom sought a humane but conservative mean. Elsewhere he implored masters to treat their slaves with Christian charity,[52] and in his first homily on Philemon he deplored the physical and especially sexual abuse that characterizes the relations between slaves and their masters: "Many have thus compelled their domestics and their slaves. Some have drawn them into marriage against their will, and others have forced them to minister to disgraceful services, to infamous love, to acts of rapine and fraud, and violence." Yet it is with the master class that Chrysostom not only sympathizes, but identifies. "These things," he concludes in his remarks on vv. 15 and 16 of Philemon, "are not written without an object, but that *we masters* may not despair of *our* servants, nor press too hard on them, but may learn to pardon the offenses of such servants, that *we* may not always be severe, that *we* may not from their servitude be ashamed to make them partakers *with us* in all things when they are good" (emphasis mine). As I have emphasized here, the preacher uses first-person plural pronouns throughout in this short but telling passage.

Chrysostom's attitude toward slaves and slavery perhaps can best be understood in the context of the conservative reaction that gripped élites in the late empire. This conservatism called for a biblical hermeneutics of domestication, an appeal to "traditional values" to shore up the crisis-ridden Roman order. Elizabeth Clark summarizes the mood:

> The spirited discussion in which ancient statesmen and philosophers had engaged concerning the ideal *politeia* was revived in Christian form by writers of the patristic era. ...The best order...they believed, was one in which a hierarchy of authority and domination obtained. Democratic or egalitarian convictions shaped their worldviews no more than they had Aristotle's.[53]

The prodigious efforts and wide and authoritative circulation of the late fourth- and early fifth-century exegetes (i.e., Chrysostom, Jerome, Ambrose, all of whom explicitly assert that Onesimus is a fugitive slave[54]), all sympathetic to the impe-

rial order, all conservative in their views toward traditionally
subordinated persons (i.e., women, children, slaves), may be
understood in this light.

Chrysostom articulates most clearly and frequently the prem-
ises and narrative reconstruction upon which the fugitive slave
hypothesis depends for its very intelligibility. He also articulates
more clearly than any contemporary or subsequent exegete that
Paul's epistle to Philemon was actively devalued in some Christian circles and that an argument had to be made for its merits
before treating its meaning. Chrysostom argues that the epistle
is of value and then proceeds to show what that value is. "But
it is useful," writes Chrysostom in the *argumentum*, "for you to
learn that this Epistle was sent upon necessary matters. Observe
therefore how many things are rectified thereby." The epistle
is illustrative of three points: first, that "it becomes one to be
earnest"; second, "we ought not to abandon the race of slaves";
third, and most important, "that we ought not to withdraw
slaves from the service of their masters."

•

The foregoing review of exegetical tradition shows that the historical reconstruction of the life situation of Philemon as Paul's
appeal on behalf of a fugitive slave can be traced back to
the imaginative and ingenious hypothesis of John Chrysostom.
What was speculation, with indications of tentativeness ("Thus
it would seem . . . ") on the part of one influential exegete, even-
tually became the dogmatic presupposition for the subsequent
tradition of interpretation. Neither the initial hypothesis nor its
later development and wide acceptance, however, is rooted in
any historical evidence.

Nor can we be certain that anyone before Chrysostom had
read the letter as he did. We have no solid evidence that the fugitive slave hypothesis antedates Chrysostom. Margaret Mitchell
has recently argued that Athanasius, Basil of Caesarea, the so-
called Marcionite Prologues to the Pauline epistles, Ambrosiaster,
and the *Apostolic Constitutions* are all witnesses to the traditional
interpretation of Philemon that predate Chrysostom.[55] The cryp-
tic reference of Athanasius, in his second discourse against the

Arians, is obscure, mentioned neither in Stuhlmacher's rehearsal of the epistle's reception history nor indicated in the indices of Athanasius's works in the *Nicene and Post-Nicene Fathers*. In arguing for the full deity of the Son, Athanasius contends that scriptural references to Christ as slave do not mean that he is any less a person of the Godhead. Athanasius asserts that those called "servant" (*doulos*) in the Bible are not to be understood literally as such.

> Thus Sara called Abraham lord, though not a servant but a wife; and while to Philemon the master the Apostle joined Onesimus the servant as a brother; Bathsheba, though a mother, called her son servant, saying to his father, "Thy servant Solomon"; afterwards also Nathan the Prophet came in and repeated her words to David, "Solomon thy servant." Nor did they mind calling the son a servant, for while David heard it, he recognized the "nature" and while they spoke it, they forgot not the "genuineness," praying that he might be made his father's heir, to whom they gave the name of servant; for to David he was a son by nature.[56]

The reference is inconclusive, but it is meaningless if not a caution against reading *ad literam* the word "slave." Athanasius argues that Sarah, Onesimus, and Solomon afford examples that militate against a literal reading of "slave," *doulos,* for it is precisely such a literal reading that has led the Arians into the error of interpreting the servanthood of Jesus as an indication of creaturely inferiority. He implies that none of the biblical characters he cites are really slaves. Athanasius refers to Philemon as *ktesamenos*, "owner" (the *Nicene and Post-Nicene Fathers* translation has "master"). Perhaps Athanasius is implying that Philemon is Onesimus's owner, but the use of the participle could be to emphasize the contrast between the owner of the house, Philemon, and the servant of the house, Onesimus. There is no suggestion that Onesimus is a thief or a runaway.

All of the other witnesses cited are notoriously difficult to date, and can be placed with certainty only in the late fourth century, thus roughly but not precisely contemporary with Chrysostom. Question 11 of Basil's *Asceticon magnum,* a kind of

fugitive slave law in Basil's monastic rule that derives its sanction from Philemon, is a variant in the manuscript tradition
of the shorter rule, and thus "indisputable dating of this text
and the tradition which lies behind it is not possible."[57] The
reference to Onesimus as Philemon's slave in the *Apostolic Constitutions* comes in Book 7, which along with Book 8 comprise
the later, presumably fourth-century additions of a composite
work that came together in the last quarter of that century. So
the witness of the *Apostolic Constitutions* is also impossible to
date precisely.[58]

If such an interpretation of Philemon was suggested to Chrysostom by earlier exegesis, Chrysostom himself is mum about
it. We know that he did acknowledge the work of other interpreters and his own occasional reliance on them. In his *Sermo
in Genesim* 6, 2, for example, he remarks "another commentator
has more exactly interpreted this and said . . . " and "Some even
say. . . . "[59] We encounter the latter phrase in the *argumentum* of
Chrysostom's homilies on Philemon to describe the detractors of
the epistle. He does not indicate in any of his homilies on Philemon, however, that he is relying on exegetical precedents. On
the basis of both external and internal evidence, it is therefore
highly unlikely that Chrysostom's interpretation is traditional.
Nor does the wide distribution of the now traditional interpretation among Chrysostom's later contemporaries necessarily make
the case for Chrysostom's innovation less credible. Chrysostom enjoyed immediate popularity among Christian intellectuals
throughout the empire. No other Greek patristic author was so
swiftly and so widely published, and more manuscripts survive
of Chrysostom's work than any other Greek ecclesiastical author.
Greek excerpts of his works found their way to the Italian penin-
sula even before the end of the fourth century, and between 415
and 419 the Pelagian deacon Anianus of Celeda had translated
into Latin seven of Chrysostom's homilies on St. Paul and the
first twenty-five homilies on St. Matthew. About three hundred
Latin editions of Chrysostom's work are known to us.[60]

On the basis of the text of Philemon, Chrysostom told a story
about slavery. There is little evidence, however, that his very
original reading was *the* original reading. The epistle's earliest

audiences, by Chrysostom's admission, were dismissive. Chrysostom's reading, strong and serious, highlighted one urgent matter, leaving other matters suggested in the text to be eclipsed by slavocratic interests. But there is another story to be told, an alternative story based on an alternative hypothesis that takes into account the epistle's truly salient elements: the familial vocabulary used by Paul to describe the relationship between the principals, his deferential tone toward the primary addressee, and the Apostle's determined and self-sacrificial concern for the reconciliation of the estranged Philemon and Onesimus. It is to these salient elements, and to an alternative reading that takes them seriously, that we now turn.

Commentary

The Text

¹Paul, prisoner of Jesus Christ, and Brother Timothy, to Philemon our beloved co-worker, ²and to Sister Apphia and Archippus our comrade, and to the church in your household. ³Grace and peace to you from our father God and Lord Jesus Christ. ⁴I thank my God as I always remember you in my prayers, ⁵upon hearing of the love and faith which you have toward the Lord Jesus and for all the saints, ⁶that the liberality of your faith may effect an appreciation of everything that is good for us in Christ. ⁷For I derived much joy and comfort from your love because you have refreshed the very hearts of the saints, my brother. ⁸Therefore, being forthright to command what's right for you, ⁹on account of love I appeal to you all the more. Being such as I am, Paul, an ambassador now also a prisoner of Christ Jesus, ¹⁰I appeal to you concerning my child, Onesimus, to whom I have become a father in prison. ¹¹Formerly useless to you, but now useful both to you and to me, ¹²I sent him to you. He is my very heart, ¹³whom I wanted to retain for myself, that for your benefit he might serve me in the shackles of the gospel. ¹⁴But I wished to do nothing without taking your opinion into consideration, so that your benefit may not be as though it were by constraint, but by choice. ¹⁵For on this account he has left for the moment, so that you might have him back forever, ¹⁶no longer as though he were a slave, but, more than a slave, as a beloved brother very much so to me, but how much more so to you, both in the flesh and in the Lord. ¹⁷If you consider me a partner, accept him as

you would me. ¹⁸But if he has wronged you or owes you anything, charge it to me. ¹⁹I Paul write in my own hand, "I will
repay," so that I not say to you that you are also indebted to
me yourself.
²⁰Yes, brother, let me benefit from you in the Lord. Refresh my very heart in Christ. ²¹Having been persuaded of
your obedience I have written to you, knowing that you will
do more than I ask. ²²At the same time, prepare a guest room
for me, for I hope that through your prayers I shall be released
to you. ²³Epaphras, my fellow captive in Christ Jesus, ²⁴Mark,
Aristarchus, Demas, and Luke, my co-workers, greet you.
²⁵The grace of the Lord Jesus Christ be with your spirit.

The Greeting (vv. 1–3)

¹Paul, prisoner of Jesus Christ, and Brother Timothy, to Philemon our beloved co-worker, ²and to Sister Apphia, and to
Archippus our comrade, and to the church in your household.
³Grace and peace to you from our father God and Lord Jesus
Christ.

¹**prisoner of Jesus Christ.** Paul so designates himself here
and in v. 9, and in remarkable contrast to his customary self-
presentation as an "apostle of Jesus Christ" (in the undisputed
letters, 1 Cor. 1:1; 2 Cor. 1:1; Gal. 1:1; in the so-called deutero-
Paulines, Eph. 1:1; Col. 1:1; and in the Pastorals, 1 Tim. 1:1;
2 Tim. 1:1). He refers to himself similarly elsewhere in the
Pauline corpus as "prisoner of Christ" (Eph. 3:1); "prisoner in
[the] Lord" (Eph. 4:1); "his [i.e., the Lord's] prisoner" (2 Tim.
1:8) — thus only in the epistles of disputed authorship. Perhaps
under the force of Paul's conventional apostolic claims, the original scribe of the manuscript codex Claramontanus reads here
"apostle" (*apostolos*) instead of "prisoner" (*desmios*). This reading
is unique: against it are all the other major witnesses that have
the text as it is rendered here. The minuscule manuscript 629
conflates the witnesses in reading, uniquely, "prisoner apostle."
A minority opinion among the minuscule manuscripts, repre-

sented by 323 and 945, read here, "a slave of Christ Jesus," another common Pauline self-appellation (cf. Phil. 1:1; Titus 1:1; on Rom. 1:1 see below).

Nowhere in the epistle does Paul refer to himself as an apostle, nor does he arrogate to himself apostolic prerogatives. As we shall see below in v. 9, where such arrogation might be expected, Paul instead appeals to his status as an "ambassador" as well as "a prisoner of Christ Jesus." Absent also are claims to apostolic privilege or, for that matter, the refusal to exercise such claims which Paul wields with rhetorical flourish in 1 Cor. 9:5. That Paul foregoes such claims here has been read by many commentators as apostolic humility, Paul's gentle refusal to "pull rank" on his primary addressee in making his requests known with an expectation of compliance. But perhaps Paul's failure to claim his apostolic credentials here, which he so readily flashes before those congregations he has established personally, is better understood as a reflection of his rhetorical situation vis-à-vis churches in which his personal standing and relationship are less than certain. For the Corinthians and the Galatians, apostolicity was Paul's trump card, which he thought he could effectively play via letter. And it is in these two congregations that Paul's apostolic credentials were compromised, or at least challenged. But for other churches that knew Paul only indirectly, his long-distance attempts to consolidate his influence could not be as bellicose as his opening salvo in Gal. 1:1. In his epistle to the Romans, a congregation that knows him only by reputation, Paul presents himself first as "a slave of Christ Jesus," and only afterward as a *klētos apostolos,* "one called as an apostle," emphasizing the divine approbation of his authority. This introduction is then followed by the traditional, quite "un-Pauline" kerygmatic formula of Rom. 1:3–4: Paul has appropriated it here presumably because it is familiar to and accepted by his addressees. Paul thus recommends himself to the Romans by first proffering his apostolic credentials and then showing himself as a new authority figure who nevertheless holds to the old traditions.

Neither the saber-rattling of Galatians nor the self-promotion of Romans figures in the rhetoric of Philemon. Paul puts forward neither apostolic pretensions nor traditional formulae to recommend himself to his addressees. It is Paul's status as prisoner and "ambassador" (on this title see below) that carries weight in his rhetorical strategy, and perhaps he has chosen this course because neither tradition nor apostolic status held the promise of persuasion. Philemon and the other recipients of the letter may not have been familiar with either: there is no hint of traditional materials or traditional ecclesiastical titles in the entire letter. Paul may have foreseen appeals to traditional language or traditional authority as abortive gestures and thus avoided using them in this letter.

Brother Timothy. Presumably the Timothy whom Paul mentions as "my co-worker" (*ho sunergos mou*) in Rom. 16:21, and traditionally identified as both Paul's junior associate on the former's evangelistic tour of Greece (see Acts 16) and the recipient of the two pastoral epistles bearing his name. He is referred to as "brother Timothy" in 2 Cor. 1:1, Col. 1:1, and 1 Thess. 3:2. As he does in Philemon, Paul conjoins Timothy's name with his own in the opening greetings of 2 Corinthians, Philippians, and Colossians. Timothy figures in a trio with Paul and Silvanus in both letters to the Thessalonians (see 1 Thess. 1:1; 2 Thess. 1:1).

to Philemon. The name appears only here in the entire *corpus Paulinum,* and only in this verse in the entire epistle. Nor does the name Philemon appear anywhere else in early Christian literature. The traditional feast day of November 22 accorded to him in the ecclesiastical calenders, and other later associations (see the appendix below, p. 71), are purely legendary and without historical basis.

beloved. *agapētos* and its cognates, which appear respectively here in the letter's greeting, the thanksgiving (vv. 5 and 7), and the body (vv. 9 and 16b), point to the challenge to Philemon's capacity to love as the issue that has occasioned his letter. The text itself is replete with the language of love in the context of fraternal relations.

co-worker. So Paul refers to a number of associates throughout his letters, and occasionally even to himself (1 Cor. 3:9; 2 Cor. 1:24). *Sunergos* is a well-established lexical item in Paul's vocabulary, appearing in every epistle of his undisputed correspondence except Galatians, where he is very much flying

solo and setting himself over and against other authority figures (cf. Gal. 1:1, 16–24; 2:1–14). As sole interlocutor with the
Galatians, Paul writes and reprimands alone. Paul uses the term
"co-worker" in recommending both himself and others to his addressees as workers who have a share with God in the labor of
the gospel. Only in Philemon, however, does he ascribe this title
to an addressee in the greeting of a letter. Paul does so to estab-
lish at the outset Philemon's relation not only to Paul himself
but to all others sharing in the work of the Lord. As a co-worker,
cooperation with other co-workers is de rigueur, part of the "job
description," as it were. In the sole occurrence of *sunergos* in the
New Testament outside the Pauline corpus, 3 John 8, *sunergoi* are
those who receive emissaries coming in God's name. "Indeed,"
says Luther, "this refers to all his fellow workers who coop-
erate in the Gospel, whether they grant hospitality or saintly
support or charity or assistance."[61] Paul here uses the term not
only descriptively, recognizing Philemon's status as a co-worker,
but prescriptively as well, suggesting the responsibilities incumbent upon Philemon as the bearer of this designation. In so
doing, Paul rhetorically prepares the way for pressing claims on
Philemon as co-worker to receive the emissary sent to him.

2 Sister Apphia. Commentators have traditionally assumed that
Apphia is Philemon's wife because her name is conjoined to his.
This speculation, like others about the epistle, apparently orig-
inates with John Chrysostom, who writes in his first homily on
Philemon, "It seems that she [Apphia] was his partner in life. Observe the humility of Paul; he . . . asks not only the husband but
the wife also. . . ."[62] This assertion, often repeated in the commentaries as well-nigh a datum of the letter's life situation, is
nevertheless without foundation on any show of evidence internal or external. Because she is mentioned among the three
addressees in connection with a Christian house assembly, it is
likely that she is in a position of responsibility in the church,
one member of the troika of house church leadership that Paul
addresses by name. If any assumption can be made about her on
the basis of the text, it is that she is an authority figure in Philemon's house assembly. Otherwise, mention of her name at the
head of the letter without further qualification is superfluous.

Archippus. Much has been made of the identification of an Archippus in Col. 4:17 with the Archippus mentioned here, especially since Archippus is one of several names common to Colossians and to Philemon (see commentary on vv. 23–24 below, pp. 64–66). Chrysostom assumes that the Archippus of Philemon and the one mentioned in Colossians are one in the same, "perhaps a friend" of Philemon.[63] Chrysostom's younger contemporary, Theodore of Mopsuestia, suggested that Archippus was Philemon's son, an inference that, though groundless, Lightfoot advances "with a reasonable degree of probability."[64] Even if a connection between the two epistles could be proven conclusively, the identity of the Archippuses in question would hardly constitute an assured result of modern New Testament scholarship. It is possible that the Archippus of Colossians and the Archippus of Philemon are two different people, that is, there may have been more than one person named Archippus who was involved in a wing of the early Christian movement within the orbit of Pauline influence. This is a minor but significant qualification in the study of early Christian documents, because, early and everywhere, figures sharing the same name were conflated in ecclesiastical memory and sometimes hopelessly confused. The tendency to fill in historical and biographical lacunae by pressing the most meager data into quasi-historical reconstruction is perhaps as strong in modern New Testament criticism as in ancient commentary traditions. For other fabulous apostolic resumés ancient and modern, see the notes on names mentioned in the concluding greeting below, pp. 65–66.

our comrade. Literally, "a fellow-soldier" (*sustratiōtēs*), originally a military term but used metaphorically by the Greek orator Themistius in the first century B.C.E. (*Orationes* 15.197c). In his epistle to the Philippians, Paul refers to his emissary Epaphroditus as fellow soldier and brother (2:25). The possible sense of *sustratiōtēs* as a technical term in the early Christian movement must remain uncertain. The word occurs only here and in Philippians; thus Pauline usage is spare and fails as an ample indicator of semantic field. Neither does the term appear in the Septuagint or the Apocrypha. *Sustratiōtēs* is an ascription from the lexicon of the root metaphor of warfare which Pauline tradition frequently appropriated in its discourse about Christian existence: Christian life is spiritual war requiring spiritual armament (2 Cor. 10:4), calling for offensive as well as defensive spiritual weaponry (Eph. 6:13–17) and martial discipline (2 Tim. 2:3). Archippus, says Luther, is "one who is appointed to battle against Satan, death, and sin."[65]

the church in your household. *oikos*, "household," is read here not only as the structure in which the assembly met, i.e., "house," but those who lived together in the house as an extended family, i.e., "household." Households were the site of several assemblies in the Pauline mission. Paul uses some form of the phrase *tē kat' oikon sou ekklēsia* to describe the household assembly of Prisca and Aquila (Rom. 16:3–5; 1 Cor. 16:19b; their house was presumably in Ephesus, if we are to trust the notice in Acts 18:2), and Nympha's Laodicean congregation (Col. 4:15; the earliest and best witnesses, B and the Sahidic Coptic version as well as Origen, agree that the name is feminine). *Oikos* and *ekklēsia* are in these instances coterminous; the welfare of the assembly is inextricably related to the welfare of the family. From the very beginning of the letter we learn that such is the case in Philemon's church. Paul's upcoming plea is as much an issue of ecclesial stability as domestic tranquility, as the matter of the letter's body shall show.

[3] **Grace and peace to you from … Christ.** Characteristic Pauline salutation combining the conventional greetings of Semitic letters (*shalom* = *eirēnē*, "peace") and Greek letters (*chairein*, "to be well," a verbal cognate of *charis*, "grace"). It appears verbatim in Rom. 1:7b; 1 Cor. 1:3; 2 Cor. 1:2; Eph. 1:2; Phil. 1:2; 2 Thess. 1:2.

The Thanksgiving (vv. 4–7)

[4] I thank my God as I always remember you in my prayers, [5] upon hearing of the love and faith which you have toward the Lord Jesus and for all the saints, [6] that the liberality of your faith may effect an awareness of everything that is good for us in Christ. [7] For I derived much joy and comfort from your love

because you have refreshed the very hearts of the saints, my brother.

⁴I thank my God always.... In the thanksgiving period of his letters, Paul expresses gratitude to God for the Christian virtues that he has experienced or about which he has heard in his addressees.

⁵upon hearing of the love and faith which you have. Variously, epistolary addressees are on Paul's mind as he prays because of their faith in Christ and love for the saints (Col. 1:3–4), or faith and love generally (2 Thess. 1:3). Paul gives thanks for the faith of the recipients or, more precisely, for the reputation of faith (Rom. 1:8; Col. 1:3–4), and their generosity in the gospel (Phil. 1:3–5).⁶⁶ He is mindful of the faith, love, and hope of the saints, in that order (1 Thess. 1:2–3, *pace* 1 Cor. 13:13!). Faith (*pistis*) and love (*agapē*) are conjoined several times in the pastoral epistles (1 Tim. 1:5; 2:15; cf. 4:12; 2 Tim. 1:13), as are peace and love (*eirēnē... kai agapē*) in Eph. 6:23. It is only in Philemon that Paul mentions love before faith, no doubt due to the importance of love in the rhetorical strategy of the letter.

⁶the liberality of your faith. Paul expresses gratitude for Philemon's reputation for generous hospitality. *Koinōnia,* translated here as "liberality," may signify partnership, joint ownership, or shared possession and is often translated as "fellowship." The word may also mean the concrete effect of such sharing, i.e., a gift or contribution and, by extension, the proclivity to share of one's substance, thus "generosity" (see *Corp. Herm.* 13.9, where *koinōnia* is contrasted to *pleonexia,* "greed").⁶⁷ The context of Philemon indicates that Paul has in mind this latter meaning of *koinōnia,* for Paul congratulates Philemon on his reputation among the saints for generous hospitality. Philemon's active liberality is born of faith, *hē koinōnia tes pisteōs,* for the fellowship of giving is faith in action.

may effect the appreciation of everything that is good for us. The word translated "appreciation" here, *epignōsis,* occurs fifteen times in the Pauline corpus (five of these occurrences in undisputed letters) and has the nuance of moral recognition or sensibility (Rom. 3:20), or appreciation, as in 1 Cor. 16:18 where the verbal form of the root is used. Paul prays that in his exercise of hospitality Philemon will effect an appreciation of "everything good," that by serving the saints Philemon may come to know what is good for them in Christ. For Paul, "the good," *to agathon,* here and again in v. 14 is not an abstraction but action realized in the concrete context of human relationships.

Paul prays not merely that Philemon would seek the welfare of those saints who come to him, as he exhorts the Thessalonians to do (1 Thess. 5:15, *pantote to agathon diōkete eis allēlous,* "always seek out what's good for one another"), but also that Philemon would be cognizant of everything that is beneficial for their community of faith. Paul's prayer is that Philemon will acquire an appreciation for the total welfare of his sisters and brothers in every respect.

7 For I have derived much joy and comfort.... Paul is comforted, encouraged by Philemon's gracious treatment of others, thus setting a precedent in the letter for Paul's identification of his own well-being with that of others in his circle of fellowship. Paul will extend this identification to include Onesimus.

because you have refreshed. In the past Philemon has afforded relief and respite to other Christians, presumably other emissaries and envoys who enjoyed his hospitality and spread the word of Philemon's graciousness in their travels. Ignatius (Smyrn. 9.13–10.1) uses the verb "refresh," *anapauō,* in his commendation of the Smyrnaeans for their hospitality toward him and his envoys: "In all respects you refreshed [*anepausate*] me and Jesus Christ you. You refreshed [*anepausate*] Philo and Rheus, ministers of God, in every way."

the very hearts. Philemon has provided respite for "the very hearts of the saints," i.e., literally, "the entrails," so in vv. 12 and 20. The entrails, *splanchna,* were regarded by the ancients as the seat of sentiments, especially compassion. A felicitous translation for this idiomatic phrase continues to challenge translators.[68] F. Forrester Church, whom I have followed, renders it as "my very heart."[69]

Lightfoot has pointed out that the term "my very heart" is a gloss for "my son" in the Peshitta, and this appears to be its meaning in *Test. Patr. Zeb.* 8: "And so in the last days God

shall send his very heart [*to splanchnon autou*] upon the earth."[70]
Artemidorus explains that children are customarily called *ta splanchna* (*Dreams,* 1.57).[71] Lightfoot notes, however, that "Paul's usage elsewhere...connects *splanchna* with a different class of ideas."[72] If Paul were aware of both meanings of the word, the "different class of ideas" may be Pauline double-entendre. Paul anticipates soliciting the refreshment of Onesimus, his own child (*teknon=splanchna*), as a refreshment of his own very heart (*splanchna*).

brother. Paul concludes the thanksgiving section of the letter with the vocative "brother," a direct address that further draws Philemon into his discursive embrace. This personalizing touch is more than gratuitous. Paul underscores what he has already indicated in the greeting by designating Philemon as a "beloved brother" (v. 2); Paul and Philemon share a working relationship of intimacy and obligation that binds them to one another, and to other "brothers" and "sisters," with familial force. Paul will let drop yet another vocative "brother" in v. 20 for the same reason, for Paul is relying on the constraining power of the fraternal bond to effect Philemon's compliance.

The Body (vv. 8–16)

[8]Therefore, being forthright to command what's right for you, [9]on account of love I appeal to you all the more. Being such as I am, Paul, an ambassador but now also a prisoner of Christ Jesus, [10]I appeal to you concerning my child, Onesimus, to whom I have become a father in prison. [11]Formerly useless to you, but now useful both to you and to me, [12]I sent him to you. He is my very heart, [13]whom I wanted to retain for myself, that for your benefit he might serve me in the shackles of the gospel. [14]But I wished to do nothing without taking your opinion into consideration, so that your benefit might not be as though it were by constraint, but by choice. [15]For on this account he quickly departed for the moment, so that you might duly have him back, [16]no longer as though he were a slave, but, more than a slave, as a beloved brother very much

so to me, but how much more so to you, both in the flesh and
in the Lord.

8 Therefore, being forthright to command what's right for you.
Paul is not commanding Philemon; the object of the verb is not
"you" (*soi*), but "the appropriate thing," that is, "the right thing
to do" (*to anēkon*). He does not dictate terms to Philemon. His
diplomatic prose throughout the letter suggests that he is not
in a position to do so. But Paul has already taken what he has
deemed the appropriate course of action in dispatching Onesimus. Paul has sent Onesimus to Philemon, and he is confident
that it is "the right thing to do."

9 on account of love I appeal to you all the more. Paul asserts
that his chosen course is more than pragmatic. There is yet a
more compelling motivation for his actions: love. Presumably
not Paul's love for Philemon; although Paul may indeed love
Philemon, his love for Philemon is the explicit basis for none
of his appeals. No doubt the love to which Paul refers here is the
same love Paul claims throughout the letter — Philemon's love
for the saints. On the basis of this love Paul makes his appeal.

Paul the ambassador. The manuscript tradition supports the
reading *presbutēs*, "old man." Philo, following Hippocrates, sets
the age of an "old man" (*presbutēs*) to be between fifty and
fifty-six years.[73] The context is patient, however, of Bentley's
conjectural emendation, *presbeutēs*, "ambassador."[74] Though Paul
will describe himself as Onesimus's parent in the gospel (v. 10),
we might expect an appeal on the basis of seniority to be pater-
nal. Nowhere in the epistle, however, does Paul entreat Philemon
as a father, nor is the letter anywhere paternalistic in tone. Indeed, the deferential tenor already noted militates against this.
The letter is throughout an exercise of epistolary diplomacy.
Paul's rhetorical tone is precisely that of an ambassador. This is
how he presents himself elsewhere in the *corpus Paulinum*: 2 Cor.
5:20, "being an ambassador for Christ"; and Eph. 6:20, where
he describes himself as "being an ambassador on a chain."[75] In
both instances it is not the noun *presbeutēs* but the verb *presbu-
teuō* that occurs. In Philem. 9, however, in conjunction with the
noun "prisoner," *desmios* (i.e., "a *presbeutēs*, and now a *desmios*")

would call for the nominal form for rhetorical balance, as Loh-meyer has argued.[76] Lightfoot's observation that *presbutēs* and *presbeutēs* were homophones in *koinē* Greek, and thus indistin-guishable to the scribal ear, is certainly correct. Thus the two words are sometimes confused in the textual traditions of the Septuagint and other contemporaneous literature; recourse to these texts to resolve the issue is not to find a solution but to encounter the problem again. Even lexicography itself may be inconclusive, for C. F. D. Moule[77] and others[78] have argued that "ambassador" and "old man" are both glosses for *presbutēs,* and therefore Bentley's conjecture is ultimately unnecessary. Ronald Hock has argued that the confusion of *presbutēs* and *presbeutēs* is comparatively rare in *koinē* Greek manuscripts, and there is no trace of confusion in the manuscript witnesses of Philem. 9: the ground of Paul's appeal is thus his advanced years, and as an old man he depends upon his child Onesimus for support.[79] But Paul is not seeking support in this letter: he is seeking a negotiated settlement of the tensions between Onesimus and Philemon. The letter's general sense as well as both the sound and syntax of its words suggest the reading *presbeutēs.*

now also a prisoner of Christ Jesus. As he does in v. 1, Paul invokes his status as prisoner, one who suffers incarceration for the sake of Christ. This status enhances the persuasive power of his plea. Early Christians were exhorted to exercise special con-cern for those in prison (see, e.g., Matt. 25:36; Heb. 10:34; 13:3), and even in Paul's time incarcerated Christian leaders may have enjoyed an elevated status in the Christian community. Such el-evated status is to be presupposed roughly a half century later in the letters of Ignatius, who attempts to translate into eccle-sial power his prestige as convict and imminent martyr. Ignatius skillfully plays this trump throughout his correspondence, and apparently to good effect. In his epistle to the Smyrneans, for example, he orchestrates the dispatch of several envoys while exhorting his addressees to continue to support him and his en-tourage both spiritually and materially (Smyrn 9.1–12.1). By the second century Christians had established a reputation for their care and adulation of prisoners. Thus Lucian's parody in his *Life of Peregrinnus,* where Peregrinnus the erstwhile sophist and er-

satz Christian prophet is excessively pampered in his prison cell
by doting Christians:

> Well, when he [Peregrinnus] had been imprisoned, the
> Christians, regarding it as a calamity, left nothing undone
> in an effort to rescue him. Then, as this was impossible,
> every other form of attention was shown to him, not in
> any casual way but with assiduity.... Indeed, people even
> came from the cities in Asia, sent by the Christians at their
> common expense, to succour and encourage the hero. They
> show incredible speed whenever any such public action is
> taken; for in no time they lavish their all.[80]

Perhaps Paul's authority, or at least his influence, had been en-
hanced by his incarceration, and he is attempting to exploit
this enhancement rhetorically as Ignatius of Antioch was later
to do. Even now as in antiquity, the imprisonment of leaders of
embattled movements may augment the prestige of those leaders and steel the resolve of their constituents. Centuries later
and closer to our own time, Martin Luther King Jr., arrested
for anti-racist civil disobedience, authored his now famous letter from Birmingham jail. Answering the criticism of moderate
white clergymen that he was an "outside agitator" interloping in
Birmingham race relations, King sets the record straight by reminding his clerical colleagues that his aid was solicited by civil
rights activists in Birmingham and invokes the example of the
apostle Paul: "Like Paul I must constantly respond to the Mace-
donian call for aid."[81] Like Paul's epistle to Philemon, King's
open letter to his white fellow clergymen deftly combined radical demands for action with a tone that was deferential and
conciliatory throughout. King makes several references to his
present imprisonment, apologizing for the "strange thoughts"
of his letter and that it was "much too long."[82] Yet he explains
that the conditions of his incarceration are the cause of his letter's quirks: "What else is there to do," he writes, "when you
are alone for days in the dull monotony of a narrow jail cell."[83]
Taylor Branch has asserted that King's letter had and continues
to have an irresistible moral appeal because "the history of the
early Christian church made jail the appropriate setting for spir-

itual judgments.... Buried within most religious Americans was an inchoate belief in persecuted spirituality as the natural price of their faith."[84] It is the ignominious jailhouse that constitutes the moral high ground which in every age must be ceded to those who suffer the loss of their own freedoms in answer to a higher freedom. Lech Walesa, Václav Havel, Nelson Mandela, Aung San Suu Kyi: in our own time, the midwives of a new moment of freedom have learned in the prison cell the patience that the painful transition of labor demands. Often, sainthood in ancient times and in modern times has been forged in the crucible of "hard time" — time marked behind bars.

It is also possible that Paul is reminding Philemon that the former's options are limited due to the circumstances of his imprisonment. Philemon must grant Paul's requests because for Paul there may be no viable alternative to Onesimus's deputation. The dispatch of Onesimus is "the right thing to do" because for Paul it is the only thing to do. As an ambassador Paul may have worked to overcome Philemon's aversion to Onesimus; as a prisoner with Onesimus as his only proxy, he *must* do so.

10 I appeal to you. Paul's repetition of the word "appeal (to)," *parakalō*, is importunate: he is making a request, not a demand.

concerning my child. Paul describes several close associates in his correspondence as his "children," *tekna*. He addresses the Galatians as his children (Gal. 4:19), and the Corinthians are children whom Paul has fathered in the gospel (1 Cor. 4:14–15). Of individuals other than Onesimus, Paul speaks only of Timothy as his child (*teknon*, 1 Cor. 4:17), and elsewhere he describes his relationship to Timothy as that of a father and child (Phil. 2:22). In antiquity the disciple was the fictive kin of his master: "If one teaches the son of his neighbor the law, the Scripture reckons this the same as though he had begotten him" (*Sanhedr.* 19, 2).

Onesimus. It is likely that the Onesimus here is the same as the "faithful and beloved brother" mentioned in Col. 4:9, whom Paul had sent to Colossae and was apparently himself a Colossian. Lightfoot[85] and others since have proffered literary and inscriptional evidence indicating that the name "Onesimus" was borne by those of servile status or background. But this association has been proven false by recent inscriptional evidence.[86] Early Christian tradition knows several figures named Onesimus: a bishop of Ephesus is mentioned by Ignatius (IEph 1.3); the bishop of Borea in Macedonia is cited in the *Apostolic Constitutions* (7.46); and, in the Byzantine "Martyrdom of Saint Onesimus," the narrative elements of the martyrdom are appropriated from the tradition about an Onesimus Leontinis of Sicily, a Christian teacher martyred during the Valerian persecution in the third century.[87] In the martyrdom, this Onesimus is identified with the Onesimus of the Pauline corpus. Such conflation of anachronistic traditions on the basis of namesake was common in martyrdom tales ascribed to otherwise shadowy figures of the apostolic age, for whom hagiography found a biographical vacuum especially abhorrent.

Paul has strategically avoided Onesimus's name up to this point in the letter, and it appears only here in v. 10, suggesting that the mere mention of his name to Philemon might prove provocative. Paul is well aware of Philemon's strong objection to Onesimus, and so he introduces Onesimus in the letter explicitly only after presenting himself as an ambassador, reiterating his own status as prisoner, and describing his own intimate relation to Onesimus.

[11] Formerly useless . . . now useful. "Useless," *achrēston,* occurs only here in the entire New Testament. "Useful," *euchrēston,* appears only twice in the New Testament, both occurrences being found in 2 Timothy, of honorable household utensils (2:21) and of Mark, who is described as "useful for ministry" (4:11). The antithesis of "useful" and "useless" appears repeatedly, as Lohse has pointed out,[88] in the parenesis of the *Shepherd of Hermas* (*Vis.* 3.6.1, 2, 7; *Mand.* 5.1.6). The contrast here is a special rhetorical construction on Paul's part, and he may be troping the same early parenetic word play current or traditional for *Hermas.* At any rate, the play on words does not suggest Onesimus's name, which means "beneficial": Paul will pun on Onesimus's name later in the letter (see commentary on v. 20 below, p. 63).

[12] I sent him to you. Paul's *modus operandi* was to dispatch emissaries as his proxies to assemblies that he could not visit personally, and one of the motives of his letter writing was to provide letters of introduction or commendation for these emissaries. Paul has made an unnatural effort not to repeat Onesimus's name in the apposite clauses that follow in v. 12, resulting in unusual word order and no small confusion among the manuscript witnesses, which testify to seven different forms of the verse. The different traditions and their witnesses, listed in brackets, are as follows. The literal translations reflect the syntax of the Greek.

A. "... whom I sent to you, him, that is, my very heart." (ὃν ἀνέπεμψά σοι, αὐτόν, τοῦτ ἔστιν τὰ ἐμὰ σπλάγχνα [Sinaiticus, A, 33, pc])

B. "... whom I sent, but you (?), him, that is, my very heart." (ὃν ἀνέπεμψά σὺ δὲ αὐτόν, τοῦτ ἔστιν τὰ ἐμὰ σπλάγχνα [F, G])

C. "... whom I sent to you. Him, that is, my very heart, accept." (ὃν ἀνέπεμψά σοι, αὐτόν, τοῦτ ἔστιν τὰ ἐμὰ σπλάγχνα, προσλαβοῦ [C*])

D. "... whom I sent to you. But you him, that is, my very heart, accept." (ὃν ἀνέπεμψά σοι, σὺ δὲ αὐτόν, τοῦτ ἔστιν τὰ ἐμὰ σπλάγχνα, προσλαβοῦ [C2, D*, pc])

E. "... whom I sent. But you him, that is, my very heart, accept." (ὃν ἀνέπεμψά, σὺ δὲ αὐτόν, τοῦτ ἔστιν τὰ ἐμὰ σπλάγχνα, προσλαβοῦ [Sinaiticus2, C2, D, Y. M, lat (sy)])

F. "... whom I sent to you. But you accept him, my very heart." (ὃν ἀνέπεμψά σοί, σὺ δὲ αὐτόν προσλαβοῦ, τὰ ἐμὰ σπλάγχνα [048, g])

G. "... whom I sent. But you accept him, my very heart." (ὃν ἀνέπεμψά, σὺ δὲ αὐτόν προσλαβοῦ, τὰ ἐμὰ σπλάγχνα [pc])

The witnesses not only testify to the awkwardness of the sentence, thus serving as an index of Paul's rhetorical artifice here, but a significant minority indicate that it is here in the letter where Paul explicitly enjoins Philemon to accept (*proslabou*)

Onesimus. Otherwise the plea to accept Onesimus does not appear until in v. 17. The UBS Committee has adopted reading A for its text because "it best explains the origin of the other readings." *proslabou*, the imperative "accept," and *su*, singular "you," were added "to smooth the syntax."[89] The permutation of the witnesses is better explained, however, by positing reading D as the progenitor of the others. The verse originally contained the pendulous *proslabou* at the end of the clause. The syntax reeks of the rhetorical situation of the entire letter: Paul conjoins adversatively (*de*, "but") Philemon ("you") and Onesimus ("him"); the pronouns are juxtaposed. Paul prefixes his intimate relation to Onesimus (*ta ema splanchna*, "my very heart") and postpones his request, "accept [him]," until the very end of the clause.

We are here at the heart of the letter, for here we come to Paul's controversial request. Paul's rhetorical contortions created problems for later scribes even as he sought to solve problems for Philemon, Onesimus, and himself. The suspension of *proslabou* is the source of scribal confusion, but not because it was added later, as the UBS Committee has surmised. The problem was not the absence of *proslabou*, but its postponed presence. From this problem two scribal traditions flowed. One tradition sought to fix the overwrought syntax. The clause is weighted for full rhetorical effect like a heavily laden suspension bridge. F and G lighten the load by placing the verb next to its object and eliminating the "that is" (which I have translated simply as "he") that introduces the apposition "my very heart."

The refashioned clause cuts to the chase; but if the flurry of appositive adjectives and relative clauses in the body of the letter is any indication of Paul's rhetorical intentions, the scribes have fixed a clause that wasn't broken. Paul purposely placed these appositives between Onesimus's name and the request on his behalf. To change the sentence is to change Paul's rhetorical intention. In the other scribal stream, the verb "accept" fell out of the clause altogether early on in the course of copying. We see this in the otherwise nonsensical reading B, which retains "but you," the opening of the clause, but lacks the verb "accept" that closes it. Witness A improves witness B by not retaining this opening; the rest of the clause reads as a continuation of the relative clause that has gone before. It's not art, but at least the clause does not demand a nonexistent verb to fill it out.

my very heart. Paul has spoken of Philemon's generous relief to "the very hearts of the saints" in the thanksgiving section of the letter. Paul now identifies Onesimus as his own "very heart," anticipating the request that Philemon afford refreshment to Paul's "very heart," Onesimus. In setting up this lexical equation, "Onesimus = my very heart," Paul avoids having to request baldly that Philemon grant hospitality to Onesimus, a request that, if so put, might prove too much a test for Philemon's good graces.

[13] **whom I wanted to retain.** The verb "wanted," *eboulomēn*, literally "I was wanting," is in the imperfect tense, indicating an ongoing desire from a time prior to Paul's request. Paul had already decided to impress Onesimus into service to Philemon's assembly before consulting with Philemon about the matter, for, as we have seen in v. 8, he was confident in the appropriateness of his decision. The compulsory nuance of *katechein,* "to retain," implies that Paul seeks to conscript Onesimus for this ministry. Onesimus's visit is initiated by Paul unilaterally, not at the request or according to the desire of either of the other principals. Paul does not say, "I want to retain him here with me," that is, Paul is not expressing a desire to keep Onesimus in prison with him. Paul is retaining Onesimus's services, not his person.

that for your benefit he might serve me. Paul's desire is that Onesimus serve him by serving Philemon. Though Onesimus is being sent to Philemon's assembly for the work of the ministry, Paul speaks of Onesimus's service to Philemon as service to Paul himself. The loving reception of Onesimus that Paul enjoins on Philemon is ultimately for the purpose of facilitating the apostle's ministry. If Paul were sending his emissary to be Philemon's slave, we would expect some form of *douleō,* "to serve as a slave," as the verb of this clause; the verb here, *diakoneō,* is used specifically in Pauline vocabulary to refer to Christian service.[90] Paul sends Onesimus to Philemon as a minister in the gospel to serve as Paul's proxy. "Both [Onesimus and Philemon] are servants for Christ's sake in the discharge of a ministry congenial to both."[91] Paul is sending Onesimus as his own representative to Philemon's church and has written to urge Philemon to receive the apostle's emissary in lieu of the apostle himself. The combination of request for assistance using forms of the verbs *sunergō,* "work together," and *lambanō,* "accept," the intimate relation of the writer to the party being recommended, and the express hope on the part of the writer that the recommended party be received by the addressees as if he were the writer himself, are all typical characteristics of the letter of recommendation for emissaries.[92] Robert Funk has identified three aspects — epistolary communication, dispatch of an emissary, and (the promise of) personal presence — as constituting Paul's apostolic *parousia,* "the presence of apostolic authority and power" Paul projects in his letters.[93] For the second element of the apostolic *parousia,* the dispatch of an emissary, Funk has delineated the following form: (a) the actual dispatch, i.e., "I send to you ... "; (b) the presentation of the delegate's credentials, introduced by a relative clause, "who is ... "; and (c) the purpose of the dispatch, explained in a purpose clause.[94] This emissary dispatch formula may be described at the same time more loosely and precisely as a dispatch clause comprised of (a) a verb of sending in the first person ("I" or "we") and indirect object in the second person ("to you"), (b) a direct object of the verb of sending with modifying appositives, and (c) a purpose clause. Of the several examples identified by Funk, four correspond exactly to the emissary dispatch formula: 1 Cor. 4:17, 1 Thess. 3:2–5, 2 Cor. 8:18, and Phil. 2:25.

> 1 Cor. 4:17 — "For this reason I sent to you Timothy, who is my beloved and faithful child in the Lord, to remind you of my ways in Christ."
>
> (a) "I sent to you" (ἔπεμψα ὑμῖν)
>
> (b) "Timothy, who is my beloved and faithful child in the Lord" (Τιμόθεον, ὃς ἔστιν μου τέκνον ἀγαπητόν καὶ πιστὸν ἐν κυρίῳ)
>
> (c) "to remind you of my ways in Christ" (ὃς ὑμᾶς ἀναμνήσει τὰς ὁδούς μου τὰς ἐν Χριστῷ)

1 Thess. 3:2 — "...and we sent Timothy, our brother and God's co-worker in the gospel of Christ to strengthen and encourage you for the sake of your faith."

(a) "we sent" (ἐπέμψαμεν)

(b) "Timothy, our brother and God's co-worker in the gospel of Christ" (Τιμόθεον, τὸν ἀδελφὸν ὑμῶν καὶ συνεργὸν τοῦ θεοῦ ἐν τῷ εὐαγγελίῳ)

(c) "to strengthen and encourage you for the sake of your faith" (εἰς τὸ στηρίξαι ὑμᾶς καὶ παρακαλέσαι ὑπὲρ τῆς πίστεως ὑμῶν)

2 Cor. 8:18, 20 — "With him [i.e., Titus] we sent the brother who is famous among all the churches for the gospel....We intend that no one find fault with us...."

(a) "we sent with" (συνεπέμψαμεν)

(b) "the brother, who is famous...in the gospel..." (τὸν ἀδελφὸν οὗ ὁ ἔπαινος ἐν τῷ εὐαγγελίῳ...)

(c) "that no one find fault with us" (μή τις ἡμᾶς μωμήσηται)

Phil. 2:28 — "Eagerly I sent him, that you seeing him again you may rejoice,..."

(a) "I sent" (ἔπεμψα)

(b) "him" (αὐτόν)

(c) "that seeing him again you might rejoice" (ἵνα ἰδόντες αὐτὸν πάλιν χαρῆτε)

According to his analysis of the apostolic *parousia* of Philemon, Funk finds no dispatch of an emissary in the epistle.[95] Yet we have seen in the examination above that Paul is sending Onesimus to the church of Philemon et al. as an extension of Paul's apostolic presence. Onesimus is being dispatched as Paul's emissary. Paul is emphatic about this in his identification of Onesimus with his own heartfelt interests (see v. 12). Once we allow that Onesimus is indeed an apostolic emissary and not merely a servile, wayward ward of the apostle for whom apologies must be made, it becomes clear that vv. 12–13 correspond to the form identified by Funk.

Philemon 12–13 (10)

(a) "I have sent back to you" (v. 12, ἀνέπεμψα σοι)

(b) "him" (v. 12, αὐτόν), i.e., "Onesimus" (see v. 10, Ὀνήσιμον); whom I was wanting to retain for myself (v. 13a, Ὃν ἐγὼ ἐβουλόμην πρὸς ἐμαυτὸν κατέχειν)

(c) "that for your sake he might serve me in the shackles of the gospel" (v. 13b, ἵνα ὑπὲρ σοῦ μοι διακονῇ ἐν τοῖς δεσμοῖς τοῦ εὐαγγελίου)

In v. 12, *anepempsa*, "I have sent back," is roughly synonymous with *epempsa*, "I sent," the first element of the dispatch formula identified by Funk (and several important witnesses indeed read *epempsa* here) in element (a). The indirect object of the clause, "to you," is here singular; it is usually plural in the dispatch formula. The chain of apposite accusative clauses that begins at v. 10 and stretches to v. 13a is element (b), in which Paul credentials his emissary by describing his relationship to him. The credentialing of Onesimus here is quite similar to that of Timothy in the apostolic *parousia* section of 1 Corinthians, where Timothy is recommended to the Corinthians by Paul as "my beloved child" (*mou teknon agapēton*, 1 Cor. 4:17).[96] The purpose clause explaining the reason for the dispatch, element (c), is in Philem. 13b, "that he might serve me on your behalf." The direct object of the verb of sending, "whom," with modifying appositives, is followed by the verb of sending in the first person, "I have sent back," and an indirect object in the second person ("to you"), which is followed in turn by the purpose clause.

The order in which the elements of the dispatch occur does not violate the formula itself, for Funk has shown that, as with other elements of epistolary structure, "Paul arrived at a consistent pattern of articulating these sections, while exercising the liberty to modify that pattern in accordance with the situation."[97] The situation of the epistle to Philemon is one in which Paul anticipates his addressee's resistance to his chosen emissary; so Paul gives the recommendation before the notice of the dispatch itself, i.e., element (b) comes before element (a). Onesimus's credentials are given well in advance of his name. By saving the worst information for last, Paul's handling of the emissary dispatch form here greases the wheels of his apostolic *parousia* and reduces friction for his apostolic envoy.

in the shackles of the gospel. Paul further qualifies the purpose for Onesimus's dispatch as Christian ministry.

[14]without taking your opinion into consideration. Paul seeks consultation, not permission. Note the Vulgate rendering of this phrase as *sine consilio tuo,* "without your counsel."

your benefit. *to agathon sou,* lit., "your good." The context does not commend reading *agathon* substantively as "good deed," i.e., Philemon's good deed, because no such good deed on Philemon's part is yet implied. The "good" Paul mentions here is the good that will redound to Philemon's benefit through the ministry of Onesimus. It is this "good" that Paul does not want to foist on Philemon.

not...by constraint but by choice. This antithetical construction occurs only here in the New Testament, though we find similar phrasing in 1 Pet. 5:2: the author exhorts elders in the community to shepherd their charges "not by constraint but willingly." The antithesis in Philemon, however, is more explicit, the contrast more pronounced. Paul is making his wishes known, but the subjunctive mood of the phrase and its modification by *hōs,* "as if," "as though," indicates that he is speaking only in the realm of possibility. It may well be, therefore, that the constraint of Paul's imprisonment makes his dispatch of Onesimus to Philemon a matter of necessity and not volition. Ultimately, the constraint, the necessity, is Paul's. This accounts for the gentle persuasion in which Paul couches his appeal, characterized by Chrysostom as "an excess of delicacy" and more frankly by Luther as "good flattery."[98] In his third homily Chrysostom describes Paul's rhetorical strategy: "No procedure is so apt to gain a hearing as not to ask for everything at once. For see after how many praises, after how much preparation he has introduced this great matter."[99] Paul says he does not want to force his preference on Philemon, but his delicacy in the letter is a strong cue that Paul is not in a position to constrain Philemon. The very attempt at persuasion, and a very savvy attempt at that, suggests that Paul at the same time recognizes the freedom of Philemon to comply with his requests and the real risk that he may not.[100] Persuasion is called for precisely because compulsion is either impracticable or impossible. Philosopher and rhetorician Richard Burke has observed, "to whatever extent the audience is free to reject the speaker's influence, we have rhetoric rather than compulsion."[101] Here, in the rhetoric about compulsion, we have rhetoric and not compulsion.

15 For on this account. That is, on account of Paul's wish that Onesimus minister to Philemon (see v. 13b).

he has quickly departed. The adverb translated here as "quickly," *tacha,* is used by Paul elsewhere only in Rom. 5:7, where it is patient of the translation "perhaps." Here, however, this translation, though commonly accepted, is much less suited to the immediate context. *Tacha* is usually accompanied by a verb in the optative and is used with the aorist indicative very rarely and only twice in the Septuagint (Wisd. 13:6; 14:19). It is otherwise translated "quickly" or "presently," and this is the likelier sense here. The verb of the clause, *echōristhē,* is deponent; though passive in grammatical form, it must be translated as active. Thus the proper translation is not "he was parted," but simply, "he (de)parted." Paul uses this verb elsewhere when discussing the separation of estranged spouses (1 Cor. 7:11, 15), where it is clearly deponent. Paul uses the verb in its transitive, active form when he speaks of separation from God (Rom. 8:35, 39).

for the moment. For Paul's use of this prepositional phrase elsewhere to denote a brief period of time, see 2 Cor. 7:8; Gal. 2:5; 1 Thess. 2:17.

that you might duly have him back. That Onesimus has left is related as fact, thus the verb of the clause, *echōristhē,* is in the aorist indicative. When Paul speaks of Onesimus's return to Philemon, however, the mood is subjunctive; Philemon's reception of Onesimus is a possibility and, for Paul, a desideratum.

The verb *apechō*, "have back," "take back," has the sense of getting back that which is somehow due or expected, thus its appearance in phrases having to do with receiving thanks for services rendered,[102] with receiving an answer to an inquiry,[103] and in receipts indicating payment in full for goods received.[104] Paul thinks it only fitting that Onesimus be received again by Philemon, for reasons he shall make clear shortly.

forever. "for a moment" with "forever" constitute yet another antithetical pair in the epistle. Paul hopes that the reconciliation he is attempting to effect will be permanent.

[16] no longer as though he were a slave. *hōs*, "as," here has the force of "as though," indicating that Onesimus's servile status is a thought or assertion on Philemon's part and not a point of fact. As the Latin side of the diglot codex Claromontanus tells us, Onesimus is to be no longer a "quasi-slave" (*iam non quasi servum*).

The word *doulos* was a term of both honor and opprobrium in the early Christian lexicon. To be a "slave of God," *doulos tou theou*, was a special designation of the superlative saints in ancient Israelite tradition. Moses (Jos. 14:7a, Josephus, *Ant.* 5.39), Joshua (Jos. 24:29; Judg. 2:8), Abraham (Ps. 104:42), David (Ps. 88:3), and, most significantly, Jacob and Israel as the people of God (Isa. 48:20, etc.), are God's slaves. Josephus on rare occasions even uses this phrase to refer to the Jews (*Ant.* 11, 90 and 101). The term *doulos* then becomes an honorific in ancient Christian literature, used to refer to saints past and present (see, e.g., Rev. 1:7; 19:2). Paul refers to himself as a slave of Christ in several letters of his corpus (Rom. 1:1; Phil. 1:1; Titus 1:1), as do other early Christian epistolary authors (James 1:1; 2 Pet. 1:1, etc.). Even a minority textual tradition of this epistle has Paul introducing himself as *doulos tou theou* (Philem. 1 according to 323, 945, *pauci*). But in the Greek language the term "slave" also signified abject subjugation, powerlessness, and dishonor. Spiq, in his analysis of New Testament slavery vocabulary, has observed that *doulos* "designates in a general fashion the man who, being in the power of another, does not have liberty.... It remains that servitude (*douleia*) always expresses a relation of dependence and an inferior, indeed humiliated position."[105] Paul's vocabulary held both these significations in a tension central to his understanding of human existence.

One of the earliest pieces of Christian hymnody that comes down to us from antiquity proclaims that it was only after the humiliating slavery of Jesus, and after his death by a form of execution reserved for slaves, that he was exalted as lord and Christ: Paul lines this hymn in his letter to the Philippians. In Phil. 2:5–11 the ultimate honor of being God's slave is achieved only through becoming a *doulos* in its common, ignominious sense, i.e., a slave *schemati heuretheis hos anthropos,* "in the human condition" (v. 7b). Verses 7 and 8 are the quintessential statement of slave status: that "he emptied himself" is nothing other than an evacuation of the will, the resultant vacuum being filled by the will of another. This evacuation is shown to be complete by the extent to which Jesus was obedient (*hupekoos,* v. 8). This obedience, as befitting a slave, is ultimate and humiliating, indeed the ultimate humiliation available in the Roman world — naked execution upon a crude wooden gibbet ("death on a cross," *thanatou de staurou*). Yet the exaltation of the slave as lord (*kurios*), the antithesis of *doulos,* is predicated upon the extremity of his humiliation as proof of his obedience. Jesus Christ has become the ultimate "slave of God" because he had become the ultimate slave.

Paul's intent here is not to make a statement about slavery as such.[106] Nor does he seem concerned to defend the theological integrity of the myth of a descending and ascending redeemer figure that may well underlie this hymnic fragment. We look in vain for christological claims about a preexistent redeemer. Jesus' self-evacuation is, in Paul's use of the hymn, exemplary. Thus any claim of archetypical uniqueness — Jesus as the "Preexistent One," as unique otherworldly envoy who, however thoroughly (yet nonetheless docetically) takes on human guise — vastly weakens the effect of Paul's appropriation of the tradition here. His concern is not christological but parenetic: Paul employs the hymn as an *imitatio Christi* argument that is explicit both at the beginning (v. 5) and at the end (vv. 12–13) of the pericope, constituting its parenetic inclusion. He both prefaces and concludes the hymnic fragment here with exhortation. Paul insists that the torturous movement from humiliation to exaltation, from *doulos* to *kurios,* is paradigmatic. It constitutes genuine Christian existence in the world, and so should characterize the relations of the Philippians to one another.

Doulos was thus an inherently ambivalent term in earliest Christianity, containing in its paradoxical semantic field the paradox of the gospel proclamation *in nuce.* This ambivalence is reflected elsewhere in early Christian literature. In the third-century apocryphal Acts of Thomas, the apostle Thomas is chosen by lot to missionize India, but he refuses to "preach the truth among the Indians." As a slave of Jesus Christ, he is nevertheless reluctant to do his lord's bidding.

> And... the savior appeared to him by night and said to him: "Fear not, Thomas, go to India and preach the word there, for my grace is with thee." But he would not obey and said: "Send me where you will — but somewhere else! For I am not going to the Indians." And as he thus spoke and thought, it happened that a certain merchant was there who had come from India. His name was Abban and he had been sent by King Gundaphorus, and had received orders from him to buy a carpenter and bring him back to him. Now the Lord saw him walking in the marketplace at noon, and said to him: "Do you wish to buy a carpenter?" He said to him: "Yes." And the Lord said to him: "I have a slave [*doulon*] who is a carpenter, and wish to sell him." And when he had said this he showed him Thomas from a distance, and agreed with him for three pounds of uncoined (silver), and wrote a deed of sale saying: I Jesus the son of Joseph the carpenter confirm that I have sold my slave, Judas by name, to you, Abban, a merchant of Gundaphorus the king of the Indians. And when the deed of sale was completed the Savior took Judas, who is also (called) Thomas, and led him to the merchant Abban. And when Abban saw him, he said to him: "Is this your master [*despotēs*]?" And the apostle answered and said: "Yes, he is my lord [*kurios*]." But he said: "I have bought you from him." And the apostle was silent.[107]

The irony of this vignette was no doubt as clear to its earliest audiences as to its protagonist. Thomas, as an apostle of Jesus Christ, is a servant of his Lord. But though he cries "Lord, Lord," he nevertheless refuses to follow the dominical command. He becomes obedient only after being literally sold into slavery to another man by his master. The apostle falls silent when he realizes that he is in thrall to his master (*despotēs*) because he refused to be a slave to his lord (*kurios*); he has become a real slave because he has failed to be a true slave. The play on words here trades on the ambivalence of *doulos* in earliest Christianity.

As we have seen, Onesimus's servile identity in traditional exegesis of the epistle rests entirely on the one word "slave," *doulos,* here. As we have also seen, as such it is the slender exegetical thread by which this tendentious interpretation dangles. The ambiguity of this word in ancient Christian vocabulary in general and in the peculiar context of this epistle in particular was noted during the American Civil War by abolitionist exegete Stephen Vail, professor of biblical and oriental literature in the Methodist General Biblical Institute of Concord, New Hampshire:

> Nor is it certain that he ever was a *slave* to Philemon or any other man. He was or had been a servant — a *doulos* — but there is no evidence that he had been a slave. . . . There is no other evidence in the text that Onesimus was a slave except what is derived from the use of the term *doulos,* but this does not imply that he was a slave any more than that the apostle Paul was a slave, for he calls himself a *doulos* of Jesus Christ.[108]

All indications here are that if Onesimus was a *doulos,* he was, like Paul and his associates (see Phil. 1:1), a *doulos tou theou,* a slave of God.

but, more than a slave. Paul trades on the negative side of the ambivalence of *doulos* here, suggesting the figure of the slave as the antitype of a blood relative. The slave, as Orlando Patterson has shown, is constitutively bereft of family relations, slavery being a state Patterson has termed "natal alienation." "It was this alienation of the slave from all formal, legally enforceable ties of 'blood,' and from any attachments to groups or localities other than those chosen for him by the master" that universally characterizes the plight of all slaves.[109]

Paul and his addressees were well aware of the reality of the natal alienation of slaves. Indeed slavery is the operative metaphor Paul uses to talk about the alienation of humanity from God, an alienation that placed human beings outside the family circle of the Father's divine economy. Orlando Patterson's characterization of the slave matches Paul's assessment of human existence under the bondage of sin. Just as the slave is, in the words of Patterson, "quintessentially without honor," so human existence in tyranny to the law of flesh is shameful and wretched.[110] Just as the slave is "socially dead," so enslavement of humankind to sin results in spiritual death.[111] And just as the slave is "natally alienated," cut off from the bonds of ancestry and progeny, so too, according to Paul, enslaved humanity is cut off from divine paternity and inheritance.[112]

Paul's awareness of the slave's natal alienation is nowhere more evident than in the fourth chapter of his epistle to the Galatians. The "poor and paltry elements" of Gal. 4:9 have been variously identified and discussed in the commentaries. But however one identifies these "elements" (*ta stoicheia*), enslavement to these cosmic forces worries Paul, for he has already established in v. 7 that the Galatians, there addressed in the singular, are no longer slaves (*doulos*) but sons (*huios*), and thus heirs (*klēronomos*). The Galatians' lapse back into enslavement threatens forfeiture of their rights of inheritance (see esp. vv. 5 and 7), for slaves cannot be heirs. Paul then launches into a typological exposition of the celebrated example of the conflict between son and slave in the Bible, the repudiation of Hagar in Genesis 21. Here Paul emphasizes that enslavement, in this case either to "law" (*nomos*) or "the elements" (*ta stoicheia*), alienates the slave from any pretensions to inheritance. Paul takes for granted, as does his audience, the natal alienation of all slaves. Owning nothing, inheriting nothing, the slave has no portion with legitimated humanity. The power of Paul's imagery thus rests in the common assumption of the thorough legal and social disenfranchisement of the slave. So when Paul exhorts Philemon to receive Onesimus no longer as though he were a slave, he is imploring Philemon to stop treating Onesimus as though he were beyond the pale of fraternal entitlements to love, honor, and respect.

as a beloved brother. Just as Paul says that the Galatians are no longer slaves ("You are no longer a slave," *ouketi ei doulos,* Gal. 4:7), i.e., aliens to the household of faith, but sons ("but a son," *alla huios*), so Paul insists that Onesimus be received no longer as a slave (*ouketi ōs doulon*), i.e., an alien to Philemon's household of faith, but as a beloved brother (*alla ... adelphon agapēton*). Here the themes of family relations and love converge. Fraternal love is a leitmotiv of the epistle: the chief addressee is the "beloved Philemon," along with Apphia, "the sister." Paul alludes to the reputation of Philemon's love and faith among the saints (v. 5). Paul is encouraged by Philemon's love, referring to the latter as "brother" (v. 7), and it is this love that emboldens Paul to make request on behalf of Onesimus (vv. 8–10). Paul has thus deliberately linked love, brotherhood, and service to the Christian community as elements of his argument for the loving reception of Onesimus.

Paul presupposes here an antithesis of slavery and fraternity that, as we have seen, is fundamental to his own theological anthropology. But this antithesis had already been well established in ancient Greek literature. In Xenophon's *Cyropaedia,* Panthea tells her husband Abradatas of Cyrus's exemplary conduct toward her while she was under arrest in his charge:

> And to Cyrus I think we owe a very large debt of gratitude, because, when I was his prisoner and allotted to him, he did not choose to keep me either *as his slave* [lit., "as a slave"] or as a freedwoman under a dishonourable name, but took me and kept me for you *as one would a brother's wife.* (6.4.7, emphasis mine)[113]

In the mouth of Panthea, Xenophon draws the contrast between the degradation of the slave woman and the honor accorded to the wife of a brother. In the following dialogue from Sophocles' *Antigone,* this antithesis is drawn even more sharply.

CREON: Was this dead foeman not thy kinsman too?

ANTIGONE: One mother bare them and the self-same sire.

CREON: Why cast a slur on one by honoring one?

ANTIGONE: The dead man will not bear thee out in this.

CREON: Surely, if good and evil fare alike.

ANTIGONE: The slain man was no villain [*ou gar ti doulos*, lit., "for he was not some slave"] but a brother [*adelphos*].[114]

The Loeb translation has obscured the antithesis between brother and slave upon which Sophocles plays here. Brother and slave signify an antithetical pair of relations, the former being accorded honor and the latter being accorded contempt. It is this antithesis that we find in Philem 16, which Paul employs to suggest the extent of Philemon's estrangement from Onesimus.

very much so to me, but how much more so to you. If Philemon is hospitable toward his sisters and brothers in the Lord, how much more incumbent upon him it is to be so toward one who is a member of his own family as well as the household of faith.

both in the flesh and in the Lord. Philemon and Onesimus are indeed brothers both literally and spiritually. They are siblings at odds with each other. Almost a century and a half ago, American abolitionist commentators concluded on the basis of v. 16 that Philemon and Onesimus were brothers. Virginia abolitionist George Bourne made this sardonic observation on the verse in 1845: "Some conjecture from the expression, 'in the flesh,' used in the same 16th verse, that Onesimus was a natural brother of Philemon, in which case there is no probability that the former was a slave, as the practice of enslaving such near relations was not common among the ancient heathen as it is now among modern Christians."[115] Bourne suggests that other contemporaries, the "some" who so "conjecture," recognized Philemon and Onesimus to be next of kin. For those motivated to see beyond pro-slavery apologetic, the language of the epistle foregrounds the true fraternity of its principals. This fraternity was true "both in the flesh and in the Lord."

Excursus: "A Beloved Brother"

Reckoning ahead O Soul
As fill'd with friendship, love complete,
The elder brother found,
The younger melts in fondness in his arms.
— WALT WHITMAN, "Passage to India"

Domestic discord was a common problem in contemporary religious and philosophical reflection, due to what pundits decried as the breakdown of family values.[116] The estrangement of family members troubled the social world of late antiquity. Philosophers and religious teachers often effected third-party reconciliations as revered arbiters in domestic disputes. The Jerusalem Talmud tells an amusing tale of a spousal reconciliation effected by Rabbi Meir, who appeals to the authority of popular magic as well as the Torah "to bring peace between a man and his wife."[117] Lucian writes that the popular first-century philosopher Demonax was renown throughout Greece as a peacemaker who quieted unruly mobs, silenced fractious partisan politics in the Athenian assembly, and "made it his business also to reconcile brothers at variance and to make terms of peace between wives and husbands."[118]

The proper relations between brothers was a special concern. The Roman philosopher Plutarch devotes an entire essay, "On Brotherly Love," to the subject. Hans Dieter Betz has compared Plutarch's concern for domestic tranquility with that evident in early Christian writings: "Both [Plutarch and primitive Christianity] recognize that a religious bond must undergird the natural status of brotherhood if lasting and proper relationship between brothers is to be achieved."[119] Plutarch was distressed over the decline of brotherly love in his own time and yearned nostalgically for the good old days of fraternal concord: "And according to my observation, brotherly love is as rare in our day as brotherly hatred was among men of old; when instances of such hatred appeared, they were so amazing that the times made them known to all as warning examples in tragedies and other stage performances."[120] Plutarch argued that the intimacy of friends was an inadequate attempt to compensate for the absence of brotherly love: "For most friendships in the world are in reality shadows and imitations and images of that first friendship which Nature implanted in children toward parents and in brothers toward brothers."[121] It is better, therefore, for brothers "to put up with the evils with which they are most familiar rather than to make trial of unfamiliar ones,"[122] reject malicious gossip about each other,[123] and forego haggling with each other over the division of an inheritance.[124] A brother's indiscretions, however, were to be met with forthrightness as well as forbearance. The conscientious brother should

> rebuke him [i.e., the wayward brother] somewhat sharply, pointing out with all frankness his errors of commission and omission. For one should give neither free rein to brothers, nor, again, should one trample on them when they are at fault.[125]

For Plutarch, the relation of brothers to one another was like that of the members of the body. The estrangement of brothers, then, was like the wound of amputation:

> When brothers have once broken the bonds of Nature, they cannot readily come together, and even if they do, their reconciliation bears with it a filthy hidden sore of suspicion ...the acquisition of another brother is impossible, as is that of a new hand when one has been removed or a new eye when one has been knocked out.[126]

Though a serious breach, a rift between brothers nevertheless may be healed, wrote Plutarch, through the intercession of a mutual friend:

> For as tin joins together broken bronze and solders it by being applied to both ends, since it is of a material sympathetic to both, so should the friend, well suited as he is to both [brothers] and being theirs in common, join still closer their mutual goodwill.[127]

Plutarch recounts trying to effect just such domestic damage control himself in attempting to reconcile two estranged brothers on one occasion when he was in Rome.[128]

The early second-century Stoic philosopher Hierocles treats at some length the care due familial relations. Family members are a valuable resource for survival in a hostile world, and the wise man does well to cultivate the good will of blood relatives. It is "pure madness," writes Hierocles, "to wish to form friendships with people who have no natural affection for us...and yet to neglect those ready helpers and allies who are supplied by nature itself, who happen to be brothers."[129] The tie that binds brothers is vital. As Plutarch before him, Hierocles argues that brothers are related to each other as integrally as the members of the human body.[130] Thus one is to deal with one's brother with gentleness and forbearance, even if he is disagreeable and profligate:

> Even if your brother should be such a person, I would say, "Prove yourself better than him," "Overcome his wildness with beneficence...." For do not even wild animals, which are by nature hostile to the human race, and are only led by force after first being placed in chains and confined to cages, do not even they later become domesticated when they are tamed by certain kinds of attention and daily food? And will not the man who is a brother...not change to a milder disposition, even if he should not completely forsake his excessive roughness?[131]

The third-century biographer Flavius Philostratus relates that the philosopher-hero Apollonius of Tyana reconciled himself to his "wild animal" of an older brother after the death of their father. Apollonius's diplomacy and tact as related by Philostratus are remarkably in keeping with the exhortations to fraternal forbearance, correction, and generosity in Plutarch and Hierocles:

> Someone said to him [i.e., Apollonius] that it was his duty to correct his brother and convert him from his evil ways; whereupon he answered: "This would seem a desperate enterprise; for how can I who am the younger one correct

and render wise an older man? but so far as I can do anything, I will heal him of his bad passions." Accordingly he
gave to him the half of his own share of the property, on
the pretense that he required more than he had, while he
himself needed little; and then he pressed him and clev-
erly persuaded him to submit to the counsels of wisdom,
and said: "Our father has departed this life, who educated
us both and corrected us, so that you are all that I have
left, and I imagine, I am all that you have left. If therefore
I do anything wrong, please advise me and cure me of my
faults; and in turn if you yourself do anything wrong, suffer me to teach you better." And so he reduced his brother
to a reasonable state of mind, just as we break in skittish
and unruly horses by stroking and patting them; and he
reformed him from his faults, numerous as they were.[132]

Similarly, in Philemon Paul attempts to reconcile the two brothers Onesimus and Philemon. By his carefully worded appeal, the
Apostle directs "an engagement of love between brothers." Paul
presses this "attachment and blood relationship" because that
troubled relationship must serve as the medium through which
Paul is to exercise his own ministry to Philemon's household
assembly.

The Instructions (vv. 17–22)

[17]If you consider me a partner, accept him as you would me.
[18]But if he has wronged you or owes you anything, charge it
to me. [19]I Paul write in my own hand, "I will repay," not so that
I may say to you that you are also indebted to me yourself.
    [20]Yes, brother, let me benefit from you in the Lord. Refresh
my very heart in Christ. [21]Having been persuaded of your obedience I have written to you, knowing that you will do more
than I ask. [22]At the same time, prepare a guest room for me,
for I hope that through your prayers I shall be released to you.

[17]**If you consider me a partner.** By calling him a partner, a
koinōnos, Paul suggests a close, interdependent working relation-

ship with Philemon, such as the one he enjoys elsewhere with Titus, whom he describes as "my own partner" (*koinōnos emos*, 2 Cor. 8:23).

accept him as you would me. Paul makes his identification with Onesimus explicit: what Philemon does for Onesimus he really does for Paul himself. This intimate identification of the writer with the recommended party is typical of letters of recommendation. It is not only characteristic of Paul's envoys, but, as Margaret Mitchell has noted, is a "diplomatic commonplace" in late antiquity, "rooted in first-century conventions for social and diplomatic relationships."[133] This commonplace is based on the assumptions that the reception of the envoy is tantamount to the reception of the one who sends him,[134] that envoys have authority to speak for those who sent them in accordance with their instructions,[135] and that often the envoy can be relied on to responsibly represent the one by whom he is sent because of an intimate relationship between the sender and envoy.[136] All three assumptions are operative in Paul's dispatch of emissaries in his correspondence.

But Paul does not merely enjoin a warm welcome for an imminent visitor. The imperative verb used here is not Paul's verb of choice when exhorting addressees to welcome those whom he has sent to them: when instructing assemblies to open their doors to his envoys, Paul uses the imperative of *prosdechomai*, "to welcome" (e.g., Rom. 16:2; Phil. 2:29). But the verb here is *proslambanō*, the same as the one used in his discussion of the "weak" and "strong" members of the Roman assembly and their relation to one another (Rom. 14:1; cf. 15:7). Paul there urges his addressees to accept one another (Rom. 15:7, *proslambanesthe allēlous*). In so doing, he is not calling for the red carpet treatment for visiting delegates. These people are members of the same community, and Paul is exhorting them to accept one another, "weak" or "strong," "warts and all." Paul demands more from Philemon than the "welcome wagon": He wants Philemon to accept Onesimus, just as Philemon has accepted Paul. He calls Philemon not only to entertain Onesimus with characteristic grace, but to forbear Onesimus, to tolerate his foibles. Paul calls Philemon not only to put Onesimus up, but to put up with him.

[18] But if he has wronged you or owes you anything. Paul speaks
of Onesimus's wrongdoing in a conditional clause: Onesimus's
debt is not a fact but a possibility. Clarice Martin has argued that
the "commercial language" of v. 18 is a part of Paul's rhetorical
appeal to Philemon and in no way establishes as a fact Onesimus's indebtedness, let alone an implied case of theft. Martin
points out that "if" (*ei*) in v. 18 introduces a simple condition
and thus states a proposition, not a reality. Paul is only propos-
ing the possibility of Onesimus's wrongdoing or indebtedness.[137]
He is not sure that there is such a debt. He is removed from the
venue of the injustice in question and defers judgment to the
wronged party on the scene. Paul leaves it to Philemon to determine whether or not Philemon has been unjustly treated. It is
for Philemon, not Paul, to assess the damages.

charge it to me. Paul knows that if some transgression has
been committed, some debt incurred, moral suasion will not
make it go away. He shows that real wrongdoing calls for concrete reparations. Reconciliation does not come cheaply; it can
be effected only when those committed to reconciliation make
good their commitment by paying what is owed. To be an agent
of reconciliation is to pick up the check, and Paul pledges to do
so here. True reconciliation requires reparations. Paul is not interested in forgiveness, and thus the language of forgiveness is
completely absent. It would be proper for Onesimus, if indeed he
is an offending party, to ask forgiveness. Paul cannot do that by
proxy. What Paul can do and must do to effect a reconciliation
is to offer reparations for any damage done.

Excursus: "I Will Repay"

Fondly do we hope, fervently do we pray, that this mighty
scourge of war may speedily pass away. Yet, if God wills
that it continue until all the wealth piled by the bond-
man's two hundred and fifty years of unrequited toil shall
be sunk, and until every drop of blood drawn with the lash
shall be paid by another drawn with the sword, as it was

said three thousand years ago, so still it must be said, "the judgments of the Lord are true and righteous altogether."
                                        —ABRAHAM LINCOLN[138]

"The white race has got a double duty to us," said Simple. "They ought to start treating us right. They also ought to make up for how bad they have treated us in the past."
    "You can't blame anybody for history," I said.
    "No," said Simple, "but you can blame folks if they don't do something about history!"
                —LANGSTON HUGHES, "Simple on Military Integration"[139]

In 1969 civil rights activist James Foreman strode like a prophet of old into Manhattan's Riverside Church and interrupted Sunday morning worship to call all of America's white churches and synagogues to pay $500 million in reparations to African Americans. Foreman was not the first, of course, to insist that some redress be provided for the ancestral disenfranchisement of African Americans due to slavery and racism. He is perhaps only one of the more colorful in a long line of reparations advocates going back to the days of Radical Reconstruction. Nor was Foreman the last. At a summit meeting of the Organization of African Unity in Senegal in the summer of 1992, American civil rights activist Rev. Jesse Jackson and Nigerian chief Mashood Kashimawo Abiola both proposed that the United States pay reparations to people of African descent on both sides of the Atlantic in recognition of the damage done by the American slave trade.[140] The proposals of the Rev. Mr. Jackson and Chief Abiola echoed similar sentiments voiced at the 1989 African American Summit in New Orleans.[141]

    The call for reparations for African Americans is no mere black nationalist innovation or invention of current radical Afrocentrism. Nor does it begin with the disgruntlement of a few ex-slaves and their progeny. Immediately after the Civil War Senator Thaddeus Stevens of Pennsylvania and Representative George Sumner of Massachusetts proposed that African American freedmen be granted forty acres and a mule to offset the enormous capital deficit they faced as newly freed proletarians without economic portfolio. The proposal was controversial from the outset. Radical Reconstructionists advocated it with a passion, but the battle for African American reparations was joined with hostility in the South and halfheartedness in the North. A compromise-prone executive branch eventually laid the groundwork for the movement's legislative demise. By the time Rutherford B. Hayes took up residence in the White House in 1877, Radical Reconstruction was all but dead, and the call for reparations shared the fate of Radical Reconstruction itself.

Though reparations for African Americans remain controversial, bristling with moral and practical complications, contemporary discussion in the New York media apparatus has been less than sophisticated in its response to the issue. In a *New Republic* article infelicitously titled "Payback Time," David Ellen claims calls for reparations are invariably associated with "separatist hate politics."[142] Ellen has in mind here the African American Summit's keynote speaker Louis Farrakhan. But on this point Minister Farrakhan's political views are no more separatist or hateful than those of Thaddeus Stevens and Charles Sumner. Caroline Alexander's *New York Times* Op-Ed piece on Jesse Jackson's proposal for reparations at the OAU Summit calls attention to African and Arab complicity in the Atlantic slave trade.[143] She argues that to indemnify America and Europe for damages is faulty historical reasoning and plays into the "popular mythology" that holds whites alone culpable for slavery. The implication of Alexander's argument is that it is somehow inherently unjust to hold accountable only the most culpable parties. If all are not indicted, none should be. According to this moral calculus, a little justice is worse than no justice at all. A corollary of this line of reasoning is that America need not honor historic injuries if betrayal was among them. These responses to African American claims for reparations, coming as they do from both ends of the American political spectrum, narrow though its band widths may be, suggest a dearth of insight into what reparations really are and what reparations really mean for the redress of injustice.

The president who oversaw the end of chattel slavery in the United States, Abraham Lincoln, recognized slavery as a moral

evil and yet was content to allow it to continue until its con-
tradictions had caused an irreparable breach in the Union. Like
his presidential predecessor Thomas Jefferson, he never believed
at any time in his life that blacks and whites could coexist
peacefully in American society. Lincoln signed the Emancipa-
tion Proclamation not to save African Americans but to save the
Union. The president's goal was the salvation not of the slaves
but of the nineteenth-century American political economy made
possible by their perpetual bondage: "My paramount object in
this struggle," he declared, "is to save the Union, and not either
to save or destroy slavery. If I could save the Union without freeing any slave, I would do it; if I could save it by freeing all the
slaves, I would do it; if I could save it by freeing some and leaving
some alone, I would also do that."[144]

With these realities in historical hindsight, the legislative failure of Radical Reconstructionists makes perfect sense. The same
nation that had grown rich by the expropriation of black labor
would now grow richer by continuing to expropriate that labor
through other forms of racial discrimination. Congress ultimately had no interest in helping newly emancipated blacks to
be competitive in the labor and other markets of triumphant
American industrial capital. Quite the contrary: the means to
achieve such an end, productive property — the ill-fated forty
acres and a mule, that economic affirmative action plan of the
nineteenth century — was the last thing thoughtful American
capitalists wanted to fall into the hands of African Americans.

Reparations, therefore, redress not only the ravages of slavery,
but also its continuing effects. American racism did not instan-
taneously vanish after 1863. Kidnapping, terror, rape, torture,
murder, "every drop of blood drawn with the lash": all these
heinous crimes were perpetrated as a matter of course under a
slave regime constituted by them. But just as important, these
crimes continued to be perpetrated in new ways long after the
disestablishment of the slave regime and its replacement by another regime just as dependent on the disenfranchisement of
African Americans. The United States benefited not only from
the antebellum slavocracy's 250 years of unrequited toil, but
from the pernicious racial legacy of slavery as well. Reparations

necessarily redress the persistent effects of racial discrimination that have perpetuated the exploitation of black labor, black products, black culture, and black bodies, from the Industrial Age to the Information Age.

Just one year before the African American Summit in New Orleans, the U.S. warship *Vincennes* mistakenly shot down an Iranian civilian airliner while on patrol in the Persian Gulf in July of 1988. Captain Will C. Rogers III, commander of the warship and author of the fateful decision to fire the missile that destroyed the Iranian airbus, lamented, "This is a burden I will carry for the rest of my life."[145] President Reagan quickly relayed his regrets to the Iranian government and announced plans to compensate the families of the 290 passengers killed in the disaster. An editorial in the July issue of *America* commented that

> President Reagan's plan to compensate the families of the 290 passengers of the Airbus is one decision that needs no debate. It should be supported by all Americans.... The proposed compensations may not do much for the victims' families, but at least they will allow the Captain's fellow-citizens help him to shoulder his burden. *It is right that they should do so*, for in a certain real sense *the whole nation, consciously or not, has been involved in the mistakes in the Gulf.* (emphasis mine)[146]

Yet there was resistance to this "humanitarian gesture," as the administration described it, on both sides of the aisle in Congress, and in an opinion poll taken two days after the tragedy two-thirds of those Americans queried said that the United States should neither apologize to Iran nor pay compensation to the families of the victims.[147] This register of sentiments led *Washington Post* columnist Richard Cohen to suggest that Americans, who are mostly white and Christian, are not terribly upset by the suffering of people who are dark and Muslim.[148]

Also just one year before the African American Summit in New Orleans, President Reagan signed the Civil Liberties Act of 1988 authorizing payment of $20,000 to each survivor of Japanese American internment during World War II. The payments are not a payback for those who lost their homes, their jobs, and, in many cases, their birthright of citizenship. Those losses were accompanied, of course, by the pain and humiliation of betrayal by one's own government. No amount of money could heal the deep psychic scars of that betrayal, which is why a third of Japanese Americans polled among the generation that suffered the internment, i.e., second-generation, or Nisei, Japanese Americans, felt monetary compensation an inappropriate redress.[149] But the Civil Liberties Act does not pretend to address in real dollars even the basic material damages of internment, such as loss of income, benefits, etc. The amount authorized is much too small a compensation for such losses. The reparations afforded by the Act are an acknowledgment that a wrong was done: driven by war-time paranoia, Americans dispossessed and locked up their own countrymen without due process and against the rule of law that guarantees the very freedoms American soldiers were fighting to preserve. The American government committed this egregious breach of civil liberty, and it was wrong. In paying reparations the United States government has recognized, officially and concretely, this wrongdoing. And so many Sansei, or third-generation, Japanese Americans, the daughters and sons of the generation of the interned Nisei, insisted that a substantial payment must accompany a government apology if the apology were to have any meaning. Said one Sansei woman, "In this country, money talks."[150]

An official, concrete acknowledgment of wrongs suffered by African Americans has never been made by any American president. America has yet to return a favorable judgment for one of its oldest open suits for damages. Until the United States government is as willing to redress African Americans as it is to redress other citizens, allies, and even enemies, the unsettled score of racial injustice shall continue to plague the damaged and increasingly insensate conscience of the nation. Paul knew well what American politicians have refused to acknowledge with respect to the claims of certain of their fellow citizens. When a debt of injustice is incurred, justice calls for the retirement of that debt. The check must be paid. But if that debt is not retired, or, as Martin Luther King Jr. put it in his speech in front of the Lincoln Memorial in 1963, if that check is returned stamped

"insufficient funds,"[151] the debtor remains morally bankrupt. Indeed, as long as the debt remains outstanding, there can be no
more business as usual. Paul must do business with Philemon,
the business of his ministry, the business of the gospel. With a
poor credit rating, his bid by proxy is sure to be rejected. And
Paul knows it. And so he is determined to redress any injustice,
pay any debt, so that his ministry may be unthwarted.

•

19 I Paul write in my own hand. Presumably Paul dictated the letter to an amanuensis but then wrote these words himself, as he
seems to indicate in Col. 4:18. Or perhaps, less likely, the entire epistle is from his own hand, as was apparently the case
in his epistle to the Galatians (6:11), unless we are to read his
words there metaphorically. A similar notice in 2 Thess. 3:17
would indicate that Paul actually wrote the greetings in all his
letters himself to endorse their authenticity, a scribal trademark
of sorts. The authenticity of Paul's correspondence is an issue
of concern in 2 Thess. (see 3:14). Paul applies his signature here,
however, to endorse his personal obligation to Philemon. Having
offered to pick up the tab, he signs his own name — an epistolary
"promissory note" — to seal the obligation he has undertaken.

"I will repay." After having recommended Onesimus to Philemon as his apostolic emissary, Paul proceeds to deal implicitly
with potential stumbling blocks to Philemon's compliance. It is
possible that the accounting terminology of vv. 18–19 (*opheilei*,
"owe"; *elloga*, "charge"; *apotisō*, "I will repay") may indicate that
Onesimus is indebted to Philemon: perhaps this indebtedness is
the very cause of the estrangement that the letter presupposes.
There is no evidence here, however, that Onesimus is guilty
of theft, as commentators from John Chrysostom on have suggested without hint of substantiation.[152] Thus it is more likely
that the accounting language is used because of the anticipated expense of Onesimus's travel and lodging, an expense that
would devolve to Philemon. It is certain that Philemon's hospitality would cost him something. That cost may have been
prohibitive, or at least objectionable, if Onesimus made an extended stay: the financial demands of Christian charity could be

considerable, and high enough to give hosts pause.[153] Paul pre-emptively counters this objection: Philemon is not to worry, for the apostle says in v. 19 that he will "pick up the tab."

Not so that I may say to you that you are also indebted to me yourself. Paul makes it clear to Philemon that Paul is offering to settle a debt, not to incur one on Philemon's part. If Paul pays the costs associated, in whatever way, with receiving Onesimus "as a beloved brother," he does not do so to make Philemon his debtor in turn. Paul is closing an account, not buying Philemon's compliance. He wants to make it clear that his offer is not a *quid pro quo,* that is, Philemon's cooperation for Paul's benefaction. He wants to settle all accounts. Paul effects reconciliation not in the language of forgiveness, but the language of partnership, reparation, and accountability.

20 let me benefit from you in the Lord. The request is under-scored with another play on words, this time an oblique pun on Onesimus's name,[154] which, as we have seen, Paul is reticent to mention. Both the name Onesimus and the verb *oninamai,* "benefit," are derived from the same root.

Refresh my very heart in Christ. Paul has already identified Onesimus as his own "very heart." Thus he is in effect repeat-ing his request of hospitality for Onesimus. To receive Onesimus is to receive Paul (v. 17), to refresh Onesimus, to show him hospitality, is to refresh Paul's very heart.

21 Having been persuaded of your obedience ... knowing that you will do more than I ask. With this expression of confi-dence Paul applies the full rhetorical pressure of his appeal, and with this confidence Paul then demands more. As we shall see, however, his earlier request concerning Onesimus's reception is subtly related to this additional request concerning his own.

22 At the same time. This phrase translates the Greek adverbial particle *ama* here. But in the Septuagint, mainly in Isaiah and Jeremiah, it often renders the Hebrew *yaḥad* or *yaḥdu,* meaning "together";[155] thus the extended temporal sense of simultaneity. The upcoming request for lodging is to be granted along with what has been requested thus far.

prepare a guest room for me. Although Paul's imprisonment has made his future itinerary more a matter of prayer than

planning, his additional request for a room for himself sig-
nals Philemon that Paul may personally inspect the fruits of
Philemon's love for his brother when the apostle himself visits
Philemon's household assembly. It would be a mistake, however,
to read Paul's perspicacity as confidence. Paul's use of the verb
"to hope" (*elpizō*) here expresses uncertainty about his future,
while impressing upon Philemon that his release is nevertheless
a real possibility. And that possibility is a tacit threat, in Lightfoot's words "a gentle compulsion,"[156] just tentative enough to
be imminent without being falsifiable. Philemon's reputation,
which Paul plays up so much in the beginning of the letter, is
at stake, and Paul implies that he may come to see for himself
if Philemon is all that he is purported to be by "all the saints"
(v. 5) and, now, by Paul himself.

The Concluding Greetings (vv. 23–24)

23 Epaphras, my fellow captive in Christ Jesus, 24 Mark, Aristarchus, Demas, and Luke, my co-workers, greet you.

23 **Epaphras.** Probably the same person mentioned in Col. 1:7
as "our beloved fellow slave" and in Col. 4:12 as "a slave of
Christ." He is otherwise unknown. Apparently at the time of
the letter's writing he was imprisoned with Paul, if we are to
take literally the designation *ho sunaichmalōtos mou,* "my fellow
captive."

Ernst Amling has suggested that the dative *Iēsou,* "Jesus," here
be read as the nominative *Iēsous,* yet another name in the concluding greeting.[157] Verse 23 would therefore read, "Epaphras,
my fellow captive in Christ, [and] Jesus...." This Jesus would
be the same one mentioned in Col. 4:11 along with the other
names of this greeting that are also paralleled in Colossians.
Though conjectural and without any manuscript support, this
emendation would further identify the personnel of the Colossian closing greetings with those in Philemon. We would expect
Iēsous, however, to be qualified in some way as it is in Col. 4:11
by the Latin nickname *Ioustus,* that this "Jesus" might not be

confused with some other person named Jesus known to the early Christian community. Because we find nothing like the "Jesus who is called Justus" of Col. 4:11, Ambling's conjecture is ingenious but unconvincing.

24 Mark. Traditionally identified with the John Mark of the canonical Acts (12:12, 25; 15:37, 39) and the Mark mentioned in Colossians 4:10 and 2 Timothy 4:11. Prior to the late fourth century no one in antiquity even suggested that the Mark of Pauline tradition be identified with Saint Mark the Evangelist. The identification of the two figures is first conjectured by Chrysostom (*Hom. I in Matt.*; *Acta ap. hom.* xxvi) and Jerome (Preface, *Comm. in Philemon*), and even Jerome does not hint at this identification in his biography of Mark the Evangelist.[158] Early tradition claims that Mark the Evangelist followed the apostle Peter as his interpreter, the first attestation of the tradition being the oft-cited fragment of Bishop Papias of Hieropolis retained by Eusebius in the latter's *Ecclesiastical History* (*Hist. eccl.* 3.39.15-16). Eusebius furthermore quotes both Clement of Alexandria (*Hist. eccl.* 2.15-16) and Origen (*Hist. eccl.* 6.25.4) as saying that it is this Mark to whom the apostle Peter refers in 1 Peter 5:13 as "my son." Tertullian claims that Mark the Evangelist's discipleship under the apostle Peter makes the former an "apostolic man" (*apostolicus*); Luke the Evangelist is likewise an *apostolicus* by virtue of his close association with the apostle Paul (*Adv. Marc.* 4.2.2; 4.5.3). Thus earliest ecclesiastical tradition recognizes at least two different figures belonging to the apostolic age named Mark, one associated with Peter, the other with Paul.

Aristarchus. Also mentioned in Col. 4:14 as Paul's "fellow captive" and in 2 Tim. 4:10. This Aristarchus is usually identified with the associate of Paul mentioned in Acts who accompanies him to Jerusalem (Acts 10:29), Macedonia (Acts 20:4), and Rome (Acts 27:2). If we further posit that the epistle to Philemon was written during Paul's Roman imprisonment, an opinion as old as the so-called Marcionite prologues of the Pauline epistles,[159] the data and these propositions may be harmonized to suggest that Aristarchus remained with Paul during the latter's Roman imprisonment, and that both Colossians and Philemon were written at this time. The Marcionite prologue for Colossians, however, claims that that epistle was written from Ephesus. But this is speculation. It remains likely, nevertheless, that the Aristarchus mentioned here, in Colossians, and in Acts are one and the same.

Demas. Also mentioned with Luke (see below) in Col. 4:14, and as a deserter of Paul in Tim. 4:10. This negative press in the *corpus Paulinum* may account for the third-century characterization of Demas in the apocryphal *Acts of Paul* 12 as an enemy of the apostle.

Luke. Mentioned in Col. 4:14 as "the beloved physician" and in 2 Tim. 4:11 as Paul's sole companion at the time. These are probably the same person, or, if either or both epistles are held to be pseudonymous, they are intended to be understood as such. Less certain is the traditional identification of this Luke with Luke the Evangelist. The argument that the two are one and the same based on the Evangelist's purported use of medical vocabulary in the third gospel and Acts was soundly discredited by Henry Cadbury in the first quarter of this century.[160] Even more dubious is the identification of Luke of the *corpus Paulinum* with Luke the Evangelist and Lucius of Rom. 16:21, put forth by Origen in his commentary on Romans (4.686). It is equally dubious that Luke here is the Lucius of Cyrene of Acts 13:1, an identification suggested by several modern commentators.[161]

my co-workers. Paul so addresses Philemon, "our beloved co-worker," in the epistle's introduction. Paul strongly suggests that he and Timothy, Philemon, and the four men mentioned at the end of the epistle are partners in a common undertaking. Perhaps co-workers are associates who are not with Paul, who are not imprisoned with him (as Epaphras clearly is), but who work with him from a distance. This is suggested by the observation that associates apparently physically present with Paul at the time of a letter's writing are not referred to as co-workers; likewise when Paul refers to himself and his associates as co-workers in 2 Cor. 1:24, it is Paul and company who are distant from their Corinthian addressees. The co-workers are operatives in alliance with and for Paul: they are his eyes, ears, hands, and mouth while he is incarcerated. Mark, Aristarchus, Demas, Luke, and Philemon are fellow laborers who are doing or at some point have done for Paul what Paul cannot do or could not have done for himself because of his imprisonment.

greet you. Epaphras et al. are said to send their regards to Philemon. The verb "greet," *aspazetai,* is in the third-person singular. There is some effort in the manuscript tradition to read the verb as a plural, and thereby read all those mentioned at the end of the letter as relaying a greeting. But this is a stylistic matter: in Col. 4:10–11, Paul introduces a plurality of greetings with *aspazetai,* thus the plural force of the verb is clear from the context. I have supplied the conjunction "and" before "Luke" for a smoother translation: the list as it stands in the Greek is asyndetic. The personal pronoun "you," *se,* is singular; thus Philemon alone is being addressed.

Final instructions to a list of addressees, a common feature at the end of Paul's letters, are absent here. Rom. 16:3–16 is the outstanding example of this feature in the Pauline corpus, where twenty-six associates are mentioned by name. A shorter list is given in Col. 4: 15, and Paul elsewhere enjoins on the addressees a general greeting "with a holy kiss" (Rom. 16:16; 1 Cor. 16:20b; 2 Cor. 13:12; 1 Thess. 5:26). Such greetings at the conclusion of a Graeco-Roman letter both widened and rhetorically embraced the implied audience. These are conspicuous by their absence in Galatians and Philemon. Galatians is a strident letter, and Paul does not want to weaken the force of his opening pronouncement (and accusations) immediately following the salutation. Therefore he dispenses with his standard thanksgiving section entirely. He leaves off personalized greetings after the stern exhortations at the end of the letter for the same reason. The epistle stands or falls on the force of Paul's passion, for he is its sole author. By his stylistic omissions he suffers none of that passion to be dissipated.

The situation attending Philemon, however, is completely different from that of Galatians, and final greetings are absent for a different reason. All the information Paul relates about Philemon is second hand, based on Philemon's reputation. In the salutation he greets an entire house church, but his letter shows that he actually knows only the three addressees by name. This suggests that Paul did not know anyone else at Philemon's house assembly; thus he knows no one to greet. Some name-dropping at the end of the letter could have further ingratiated Paul to his addressees; that he does not name names most likely means that Paul was not acquainted with the other congregants of Philemon's house assembly. Paul does not know his addressees that well, and so measures his words with "an excess of delicacy" and "good flattery."

The Benediction (v. 25)

25 The grace of the Lord Jesus Christ be with your spirit.

A characteristic Pauline benediction, as found verbatim in Phil. 4:23 and Gal. 6:18, which adds "...brothers. Amen." The final benediction in Philemon also reads "Amen" in Sinaiticus, and other uncial, versional, and patristic witnesses. "Your," *humōn*, is plural: Paul addresses his benediction to all of the letter's recipients. Thus the opening and the closing of the letter acknowledge the plurality of addressees. This plurality remains less than implicit throughout the body of the letter, in which Paul speaks to the second-person singular. Only in a medieval witness to the Old Latin (it^gig) does the text read the singular. Witnesses that read here "our spirit" instead of "your spirit," text-critically important though some of them may be, may be discounted. The second-person plural pronoun, *humōn*, and the first-person plural personal pronoun, *hēmōn*, were pronounced identically in Greek by the beginning of the Common Era. Thus these two words became confused in the course of scribal dictation. The residuum of this confusion is carried over into many Latin manuscripts, the Syriac Peshitta, and the Latin patristic witness Ambrosiaster.

The letter ends as it began —with grace, *charis* —but also with a difference. The *charis* Paul invokes at the opening of the letter is from God the Father and the Lord Jesus Christ: it is God's manifest mercy, kindness, good will. It is grace *from* God, *apo theou*, that the recipients of the letter have received and may yet receive. The *charis* of the final benediction, however, is the grace *of* the Lord Jesus Christ, the grace that is his character. It is the graciousness of Jesus Christ. Paul prays that the Lord's spirit of graciousness be with Philemon, in Whitman's words, that he be "filled with friendship, love complete." Paul prays that the graciousness that was in Christ Jesus be found in Philemon, that Onesimus upon his arrival might find that graciousness in his estranged brother, their reconciliation a "reckoning ahead... / As fill'd with friendship, love complete / The elder brother found / the younger melts in fondness in his arms."

Conclusion

The history of the interpretation of Paul's letter to Philemon is the history of a story, the story of Paul the great apostle interceding on behalf of a thieving slave in flight from his noble master. It is the "once-upon-a-time-there-was-a-slave-named-Onesimus" story, with a moral commending genteel despotism and servile obedience.

In this commentary, however, I tell another story, with a different moral.

Once upon a time there was a man named Paul. He had a colleague named Philemon, who worked together with him in the service of their common lord, Jesus Christ. Philemon had a brother named Onesimus, whom Philemon despised because of some past injustice for which Onesimus had failed to compensate him.

One day Paul was thrown into prison, and so could no longer work with Philemon on their common project ordered by their common lord. But Paul wanted very badly to help Philemon and the others working with him at his house. Incarcerated and in chains, Paul had no alternative but to send a surrogate. Having no one else to send, he decided to dispatch Philemon's brother Onesimus, who happened to be close at hand. But knowing the seriousness of Philemon's estrangement from his brother, he also decided to write Philemon a letter. Paul wrote that he was sending a surrogate to work in his stead. He wrote that the surrogate would be Onesimus, whom Paul loved like a son. He wrote that he, Paul, would pay the damages for Onesimus's past injustices. And he wrote that he, Paul, would see Philemon later, though he was not sure just when, and at that time he would pay Philemon in full. Finally, he signed the letter himself. He then sent the letter, and Onesimus, to Philemon, confident that love would correct everything, for "justice at its best is love correcting everything that stands against love."[162]

Appendix

Subscriptions

The following are subscriptions, explanatory blurbs provided anonymously at the end of the epistle by later editors and copyists. These are conveniently listed with Greek text and exhaustive lists of their respective manuscript witnesses in Metzger's *Textual Commentary*.[163] I provide the subscriptions for the Greek witnesses here, with English translation, and I have indicated in brackets the date of the earliest witness to give the reader a sense of the *terminus ad quem* for the subscription in question.

1. "To Philemon." (πρὸς Φιλήμονα) Sinaiticus [fourth century].

2. "It was completed for Philemon." (πρὸς Φιλήμονα ἐπληρώθη) D [fifth/sixth century].

3. "To Philemon and Apphia masters of Onesimus and to Archippus the deacon of the church, written from Rome by way of Onesimus the house servant." (πρὸς Φιλήμονα καὶ Ἀπφίαν δεσπότας Ὀνισήμου [sic] καὶ πρὸς Ἄρχιππον διάκονον τῆς ἐκκλησίας ἐγράφη ἀπὸ Ρώμης διὰ Ὀνησίμον οἰκέτου) Euthalius[ms] [fifth century church father].

4. "He was writing to Philemon from Rome." (πρὸς Φιλήμονα ἐγράφει ἀπὸ Ρώμης) P [i.e., numerical designation 025, ninth century].

5. "Written to Philemon from Rome by way of Onesimus, a house servant." (πρὸς Φιλήμονα ἐγράφη ἀπὸ Ρώμης διὰ Ὀνησίμου οἰκέτου) K [i.e., numerical designation 018, ninth century].

6. "Epistle of the holy apostle Paul to Philemon and Apphia masters of Onesimus and to Archippus the deacon of the church in Colossae; written from Rome by way of Onesimus

the house servant." (τοῦ ἁγίου ἀποστόλου Παύλου ἐπιστολὴ πρὸς Φιλήμονα καὶ Ἀπφίαν δεσπότας τοῦ Ὀνησίμου καὶ πρὸς Ἄρχιππον τὸν διάκονον τῆς ἐν Κολοσσαῖς ἐκκλησίας ἐγράφη ἀπὸ Ρώμης διὰ Ὀνησίμου οἰκέτου) L [i.e., numerical designation 020, ninth century].

7. "Written to Philemon from Rome by way of Onesimus." (πρὸς Φιλήμονα εγράφη ἀπὸ Ρώμης διὰ Ὀνησίμου 1927 [tenth century].

8. "To Philemon and Apphia masters of Onesimus and to Archippus the deacon of the church in Colossae; written from Rome by way of Onesimus the house servant." (πρὸς Φιλήμονα καὶ Ἀπφία δεσπότας τοῦ Ὀνησίμου καὶ πρὸς Ἄρχιππον τὸν διάκονον τῆς ἐν Κολοσσαῖς ἐγράφη ἀπὸ Ρώμης διὰ Ὀνησίμου οἰκέτου) 101 [eleventh century].

9. "To Philemon and Apphia masters of Onesimus and to Archippus deacon of the church, written from Rome from the person of Paul and Timothy by way of Onesimus, a house servant. But indeed also the blessed became a martyr in the city of the Romans, who suffered the sentence of martyrdom during the tenure of Tertullus the provincial administrator at that time, who commanded the breaking of his legs." (πρὸς Φιλήμονα καὶ Ἀπφία δεσπότας Ὀνισήμου ὅιχ καὶ πρὸς Ἄρξιππον διάκονον τῆς ἐκκλησίας ἐγράφη ἀπὸ Ρώμης ἐκ προσώπου Παύλου καὶ Τιμοθέου διὰ Ὀησίμου οἰκέτου ἀλλὰ δὴ καὶ μάρτυς Χριστοῦ γεγένηται ὁ μακάριος Ὀνήσιμος ἐν τῇ Ρωμαίων πόλει ἐπὶ Τερτούλλου τοῦ τηνικαῦτα τὴν ἐπαρχικὴν ἐξουσίαν διέποντος τῇ τῶν σκέλων κλάσει τήν ψῆφον ὑπομείνας τοῦ μαρτυρίου) 42 [eleventh century] (390)

This subscription reflects the account given in the Byzantine "Martyrdom of Saint Onesimus," which recounts that Onesimus was arraigned under the administration of a Tertullus, who concluded his torture of Onesimus with the command that the martyr's legs be broken.[164]

Notes

Introduction

1. In Albert Raboteau, *Slave Religion: The "Invisible Institution" in the Antebellum South* (Oxford: Oxford University Press, 1982), 139.

2. Herbert G. May and Bruce M. Metzger, eds., *The Oxford Annotated Bible* (New York and Oxford: Oxford University Press, 1962), 1451.

3. Richard Allen, *Life Experiences and Gospel Labors,* introduction by George A. Singleton (1793; reprint: New York and Nashville: Abingdon, 1960), 25.

4. For a critical summary of modern scholarship on Paul, Philemon, and slavery, see Neil Elliott, *Liberating Paul: The Justice of God and the Politics of the Apostle* (Maryknoll, N.Y.: Orbis, 1994), 40–52.

5. Norman Petersen, *Rediscovering Paul: Philemon and the Sociology of Paul's Narrative World* (Philadelphia: Fortress Press, 1985), 5.

6. Gervase Corcoran, "Slavery and the New Testament," *Milltown Studies* 1, no. 5 (1980): 40.

7. Richard Lehmann, *Épître à Philemon: Le Christianisme primitif et l'esclavage* (Geneva: Labor et Fides, 1978), 25 (translation mine).

8. The violent punishment of slaves was stipulated in Roman law. See, e.g., *Digest* 7.1.1.17. On the primary importance of whipping and other abusive and degrading punishments in all slave regimes generally, see Orlando Patterson, *Slavery and Social Death* (Cambridge, Mass.: Harvard University Press, 1982), 3–4.

9. For example, a sound public drubbing, the *verberatio,* was a punishment inflicted on lower-class violators lacking the wherewithal to pay punitive fines. Only the lower registers were subject to this humiliating penalty.

10. John Knox, *Philemon among the Letters of Paul* (New York: Abingdon, 1935).

11. For a brief account of the demolition of Knox's theory, see Eduard Lohse, *A Commentary on the Epistle to the Colossians and Philemon,* ed. Helmut Koester, trans. William Doehlman and Robert J. Karris (Philadelphia: Fortress Press, 1971), 186–87, esp. nn. 1 and 2.

12. Peter Lampe, "Keine Sklavenflucht des Onesimus," *Zeitschrift für neutestamentliche Wissenschaft* 76 (1985): 135–37.

13. Sarah Winter, "Paul's Letter to Philemon," *New Testament Studies* 33 (1987): 1–15. For what Winter herself refers to as the "hermeneutical component" of her work on Philemon, see her "Methodological Observationas on a New Interpretation of Paul's Letter to Philemon," *Union Seminary Quarterly Review* 39 (1984): 203–12.

14. Lampe, "Sklavenflucht," 136.

15. Ibid., 137.

16. Winter, "Letter," 3.

17. Text and translation in Adolph Deissmann, *Light from the Ancient East,* trans. Lionel R. M. Strachman (London, New York, and Toronto: Hodder & Stoughton, 1911), 205–6. Slightly modified.

18. Elsewhere (Allen Callahan, "Paul's Epistle to Philemon: Toward an Alternative Argumentum," *Harvard Theological Review* 86, no. 4 [1993]: 359), I stated that Grotius was the first to read Pliny's letter as a parallel for Philemon. I stand corrected by the summary of interpretive history in Marion Soards, "Some Neglected Theological Dimensions of Paul's Letter to Philemon," *Perspectives in Religious Studies* 17, no. 3 (1990): 210, n. 12.

19. Noted by Peter Stuhlmacher, *Der Brief an Philemon* (Neukirchen-Vluyn: Neukirchener Verlag, 1981), 61.

20. Text in Lohse, *Colossians and Philemon,* 196–97, n. 2 (translation mine).

21. F. Forrester Church, "Rhetorical Structure and Design in Paul's Letter to Philemon," *Harvard Theological Review* 71 (1978): 19.

22. Knox, *Philemon,* 20 (emphasis mine).

23. John G. Nordling, "Onesimus Fugitivus: A Defense of the Runaway Slave Hypothesis in Philemon" *Journal for the Study of the New Testament* 41 (1991): 101.

24. Ibid., 100.

25. Lehmann, *Épître,* 25.

26. J. B. Lightfoot, *Saint Paul's Epistles to the Colossians and Philemon* (London and New York: Macmillan, 1875), 310.

27. Roman law recognized slave flight from torture and other abuse as a common problem (*Digest* 21.1.23). W. W. Buckland, *The Roman Law of Slavery* (Cambridge: Cambridge University Press, 1908; reprint: New York: AMS Press, 1969), 58, has noted that "*fugitivi* were a great administrative difficulty" of the empire. Nordling, "Onesimus," 106, after reviewing ample papyri and inscriptions, concludes that runaway slaves were "a grave social problem" of the Graeco-Roman world. And art imitated life on this point during the Principate. In *Leucippe and Clitophon,* the second-century novel by Achilles Tatius, the slave girl Clio flees upon hearing that her mistress is planning to torture her

to obtain information about the intrigues of the mistress's daughter. Before absconding, Clio declares that she would kill herself before submitting to the rack (II.26). The Roman jurists had been constrained to recognize slave suicide as the ultimate flight (*Digest* 21.1.17.4). See also Moses Finley, *Ancient Slavery and Modern Ideology* (London: Chatto and Windus, 1980), 72.

28. Patterson, *Slavery,* 90.

29. Ibid., 96.

30. Stanley Elkins, *Slavery: A Problem in American Institutional and Economic Life* (Chicago: University of Chicago Press, 1959), 82. As my remarks imply, I do not agree with Elkins's assertions that the "Sambo" stereotype is peculiar to the American slavocracy and that, on the basis of psycho-historical analysis, the stereotype may be shown to have some foundation in fact. Elkins's conceptualization of the slave was roundly criticized by novelist and essayist Ralph Ellison: "Contrary to some, I feel that our experience as a people involves a great deal of heroism. From one perspective, slavery was horrible and brutalizing. It is said that, 'Those Africans were enslaved, they died in the 'middle passage,' they were abused, their families were separated, they were whipped, they were raped, ravaged, and emasculated.' And the Negro writer is tempted to agree. 'Yes! God damn it, wasn't that a horrible thing!' But he sometimes agrees to the next step, which holds that slaves had very little humanity because slavery destroyed it for them and their descendents. That's what the Stanley M. Elkins 'Sambo' argument implies. But despite the historical past...from *my* perspective there is something further to say. I have to *affirm* my forefathers and I *must* affirm my parents or be reduced in my own mind to a white man's inadequate — even if unprejudiced — conception of human complexity" ("A Very Stern Discipline," in *The Collected Works of Ralph Ellison,* ed. John Callahan [New York: Modern Library, 1995], 736–37). For a confutation of the errors in Elkins's important work, along with a recognition and characterization of its importance, see Eugene Genovese, "Rebelliousness and Docility in the Negro Slave: A Critique of the Elkins Thesis," originally published in *Civil War History* 13 (December 1966): 293–314; republished in *In Red and Black: Marxian Explorations in Southern and Afro-American History* (New York: Pantheon, 1971), 73–101. In modern New Testament scholarship, John Knox (*Philemon,* 10) has recognized the standard characterization of the runaway slave as stereotypical.

31. Lightfoot, *Saint Paul's Epistles to the Colossians and Philemon,* 308–9.

32. G. H. R. Horsley, *New Documents Illustrating Early Christianity* 4 (North Ryde, Australia: Ancient History Documentary Research Centre, Macquarie University, 1982), no. 96.

33. Garry Wills, *Under God: Religion and American Politics* (New York: Simon and Schuster, 1990), 196.

34. Larry Morrison, "The Religious Defense of American Slavery before 1830," *Journal of Religious Thought* 37, no. 2 (1980–81): 19.

35. [Frederick Dalcho], *Practical Considerations Founded on the Scriptures, Relative to the Slave Population of South Carolina by a South Carolinian* (Charleston: A. E. Miller, 1823), 20–21; see *Richmond Enquirer,* December 3, 1819; cited in Morrison, "Religious Defense," 20. See also Caroline L. Shanks, "The Biblical Anti-Slavery Argument of the Decade 1830–1840" in Paul Finkelman, ed., *Religion and Slavery* (New York: Garland Publishing, 1989), 133.

36. George Bourne, *A Condensed Anti-Slavery Argument* (New York: S. W. Benedict, 1845), 82.

37. John Gregg Fee, *An Anti-Slavery Manual* (Mayville, Ky., 1848; reprint: New York: Arno Press and New York Times, 1969), 112.

38. *Patrologia Graeca* 14, 1305–8.

39. Werner Georg Kümmel, *Introduction to the New Testament,* trans. A. J. Mattill Jr. (New York and Nashville: Abingdon, 1966), 353.

40. F. C. Baur, *Paul the Apostle of Jesus Christ,* trans. A. Menzies (Edinburgh: Williams and Norgate, 1873–75), 2:84.

41. *Comm. in Philem.* praef., in Lightfoot, *Saint Paul's Epistles to the Colossians and Philemon,* 315, n. 2 (translation mine).

42. See Theodore of Mopsuestia, *Theodori Episcopi Mopsuesteni in Beati Pauli Commentarii* (Cambridge: Cambridge University Press, 1880–82), 2:258–85.

43. Lightfoot, *Saint Paul's Epistles to the Colossians and Philemon,* 382–83.

44. Handley C. G. Moule, *Colossians and Philemon Studies: Lessons in Faith and Holiness* (London: Pickering and Inglis Ltd., 1930), 281–82.

45. *Patrologia Graeca* 62, 700 (translation mine).

46. See Stuhlmacher, *Der Brief,* 58.

47. *Patrologia Graeca* 62, 699.

48. Henry Chase, *Chrysostom: A Study in the History of Biblical Interpretation* (Cambridge: Deighton Bell and Co.; London: George Bell and Sons, 1887), 178.

49. The use of *phasi* (φασί) may connote not only oral but written materials. See G. M. Lee, "Eusebius on Saint Mark and the Beginnings of Christianity in Egypt," *Studia Patristica* 12 (1975): 425–27.

50. Some ancient witnesses to the *corpus Paulinum* show Philemon to be the runt of the letters, as it were. The Coptic manuscript tradition consistently placed Philemon last in its collection of the Pauline corpus. Cf. P. Bellet, "Analecta Coptica," *Catholic Bible Quarterly* 40 (1978): 44. Philemon was almost certainly the last of the epistles in the earliest

witness to the corpus we possess, P46, though the epistle, along with 2 Thessalonians, is now missing. In descending order of length, 2 Thessalonians would have immediately preceded Philemon, and thus the two epistles probably comprised the "tail end" of the corpus.

51. *Nicene and Post-Nicene Fathers,* 1, 6.546.

52. See for example, Hom. in Eph. 2.2, *Patrologia Graeca* 62, 157.

53. Elizabeth A. Clark, *Jerome, Chrysostom and Friends.* (New York and Toronto: Edwin Mellen Press, 1979), 1.

54. Cf. Nordling, "Onesimus," 118, n. 1.

55. Margaret Mitchell, "John Chrysostom on Philemon: A Second Look" *Harvard Theological Review* 88, no. 1 (1995): 145–47.

56. The English text is from *Nicene and Post-Nicene Fathers,* second series; ed. Phillip Schaff and Henry Wace (Grand Rapids, Mich.: Eerdmans, 1978), 4:349–50. The Greek text is given in William Bright, ed., *The Orations of Saint Athanasius against the Arians* (Oxford: Clarendon Press, 1873), 71.

57. Mitchell, "Chrysostom," 20, n. 38.

58. Ibid., 21, n. 41.

59. *Patrologia Graeca* 54, 606.

60. On the widespread reception of Chrysostom's work, see Chrysostomus Baur, *John Chrysostom and His Time,* trans. Sr. M. Gonzaga (London: Sands, 1959), 2. 470–71.

Commentary

61. Martin Luther, "Lecture on Philemon," in *Luther's Works,* ed. Jaroslav Pelikan (St. Louis: Concordia Publishing House, 1955), 29:94.

62. *Nicene and Post-Nicene Fathers,* ed. Philip Schaff (New York: Christian Literature Company, 1889), 7.457.

63. *isōs filon,* Homily 1.

64. J. B. Lightfoot, *Saint Paul's Epistles to the Colossians and Philemon* (London: Macmillan, 1875), 374.

65. Luther, *Works,* 29.95.

66. On *koinōnia* as "liberality" or "generosity" see p. 28.

67. "As the Sixth Power, I call to us Unselfishness [*koinōnia*], the opponent of Covetousness [*pleonexia*]" (text in *Hermetica,* ed. and trans. Walter Scott [Boston: Shambhala, 1985], 1.244 [Greek text], 1.245 English translation).

68. The New Revised Version of the Segond Bible replaces the previous gloss of the old version, "mes propres entrailles" (akin to the King James Version rendering, "mine own bowels"), with "une partie de moi-méme." See John Ellington, "La Bible Segond et la Nouvelle Version Segond Revisée," *The Bible Translator* 31 (1980): 138. For an ac-

count of Mandarin Chinese glosses, see Douglas Lancashire et al., "The Bible in Modern Chinese," *The Bible Translator* 11 (1960): 108.

69. F. Forrester Church, "Rhetorical Structure and Design in Paul's Letter to Philemon," *Harvard Theological Review* 71 (1978): 24.

70. Lightfoot, *Saint Paul's Epistles to the Colossians and Philemon*, 406–7.

71. Ibid. Lightfoot gives the Greek texts of *Test. Patr. Zeb.* 8, *Dreams* i.44, and v. 57. Translations are my own.

72. Ibid., 407.

73. *Op. Mund.*, 105.

74. The reading "ambassador" has numerous supporters. E.g., C. F. D. Moule, *The Epistles of Paul the Apostle to the Colossians and Philemon* (Cambridge: Cambridge University Press, 1957), 144; U. Wickert, "Der Philemonbrief — Privatbrief oder apostolisches Schreiben?" *Zeitschrift für neutestamentliche Wissenschaft* 52 (1961): 235; F. Forrester Church, "Structure," 25, n. 41. See the cogent argument for this reading based on Pauline usage and rhetorical context of Philemon put forward by Norman Petersen, *Rediscovering Paul*, 125–28.

75. Lightfoot, *Saint Paul's Epistles to the Colossians and Philemon*, 337.

76. E. Lohmeyer, *Die Briefe an die Philipper, an die Kolosser und an Philemon*, Kritisch-exegetischer Kommentar über das Neue Testament 9 (Göttingen: Vandenhoeck & Ruprecht, 1964), 185.

77. Moule, *Epistles*, 144.

78. See, e.g., Gunther Bornkamm, *Theological Dictionary of the New Testament* 6, 683, n. 2.

79. Ronald F. Hock, "A Support for His Old Age: Paul's Plea on Behalf of Onesimus," in *The Social World of the First Christians: Essays in Honor of Wayne Meeks*, ed. L. Michael White and O. Larry Yarbrough (Minneapolis: Fortress, 1995), 67–81.

80. Lucian, 12, 13, Harmon, 13, 15.

81. "Letter from Birmingham Jail." For the full text of the letter, see *A Testament of Hope*, ed. James Melvin Washington (San Francisco: Harper and Row, 1986), 289–302; citation, 290.

82. *A Testament of Hope*, 302.

83. Ibid.

84. Taylor Branch, *Parting the Waters* (New York: Simon and Schuster, 1988), 740.

85. Lightfoot, *Saint Paul's Epistles to the Colossians and Philemon*, 308–9.

86. See n. 32, p. 75 above.

87. Craig L. Hanson, "A Greek Martyrdom Account of St. Onesimus, *Greek Orthodox Theological Review* 22, no. 3 (1977): 324; English translation, 325.

88. Lohse, *Commentary,* 200, n. 35.

89. Bruce M. Metzger, *A Textual Commentary on the Greek New Testament* (New York: United Bible Societies, 1971), 657–58.

90. The verb "must refer to the Christian ministry" (Winter, "Paul's Letter," 9).

91. Marvin R. Vincent, *A Critical and Exegetical Commentary on the Epistles of the Philippians and to Philemon,* International Critical Commentary (Edinburgh: T. & T. Clark; New York: Scribner's Sons, 1897), 186–87.

92. See Abraham Malherbe, *Social Aspects of Early Christianity* (Philadelphia: Fortress, 1983), 102, 103.

93. Robert Funk, "The Apostolic Parousia: Form and Significance," in *Christian History and Interpretation,* ed. W. R. Farmer, C. F. D. Moule, and R. R Niebuhr (Cambridge: Cambridge University Press, 1974), 249. In the main I find Funk's analysis persuasive and illuminating, as will become clear in my treatment to follow. Important to keep in mind, however, are the correctives to Funk's treatment offered by Margaret Mitchell ("New Testament Envoys in the Context of Greco-Roman Diplomatic and Epistolary Conventions: The Example of Timothy and Titus," *Journal of Biblical Literature* 3, no. 4 (1992): 641–52; see esp. 641–44). I agree with Mitchell that Paul's letters and emissaries were not necessarily "inadequate substitutes" for his personal presence, but may have been deployed "because of the relative ineffectiveness of Paul's presence and his own creative recognition of that limitation" (Mitchell, "Envoys," 642).

94. Funk, "Parousia," 252.

95. Ibid., 253.

96. Funk points this out in his analysis of 1 Cor. 4:17, ibid., 255.

97. Ibid., 258; see 255–58 for analyses of pertinent pericopae.

98. Chrysostom, *Homily* II, 550; Luther, *Works,* 98.

99. Chrysostom, *Homily* III, 554.

100. On this important point of persuasion and rhetoric, see Henry Johnstone Jr., "Some Reflections on Argumentation," in *Philosophy, Rhetoric, and Argumentation* (University Park: Pennsylvania State University Press, 1965), 1–9.

101. Richard Burke, "Rhetoric, Dialectic, and Force" *Philosophy and Rhetoric* 7, no. 3 (1974): 157.

102. Callimachus, *Epigrams* 51.

103. Aeschines, *Embassy* 2.50.

104. The sense implied by Paul himself in Phil. 4:18, where *apechō* means "I am paid in full."

105. "Il désigne d'une façon générale l'homme qui étant au pouvoir d'un autre, n'a pas sa liberté.... Il reste que la servitude (*douleia*) ex-

prime toujours un rapport de dépendance et une position subalterne, voire humilée.... "

106. As Sheila Briggs has observed, "Phil. 2:7b is not about slavery as a social institution. It does not provide a critique of or apology for slavery, nor does it attribute cosmic or soteriological significance to that institution through its description of Christ taking on the form of a slave" ("Can an Enslaved God Liberate? Hermeneutical Reflections on Philippians 2:6-11," Katie Geneva Cannon, guest ed., Elisabeth Schüssler Fiorenza, ed. *Semeia 47: Interpretation for Liberation* [Atlanta: Scholars Press, 1989], 143).

107. Edgar Hennecke and Wilhelm Schneemelcher, eds., *New Testament Apocrypha,* trans. A. J. B. Higgins et al., 2 vols. (Philadelphia: Westminster, 1963-66), 2:339-40, slightly emended. The Greek text is printed in *Acta Apostolorum Apocrypha,* ed. Maximilian Bonnet (Leipzig: Hermann Mendelssohn, 1903; reprint: Hildesheim, Zurich, New York: Georg Olms, 1990), 2.2.101-2.

108. Stephen M. Vail, *The Bible against Slavery* (Concord, N.H.: Fogg, Hadley and Co., Printers, 1864), 62.

109. Orlando Patterson, *Slavery and Social Death* (Cambridge, Mass.: Harvard University Press, 1982), 13.

110. Rom. 7:16-21; 8:18-24; Gal. 4:5-9. On the social and ideological importance of dishonor as a defining characteristic of the slave in all slavocracies, see Patterson, *Slavery,* 77-101.

111. Rom. 7:20-23.

112. Gal. 4.

113. Xenophon, *Cyropaedia,* trans. Walter Miller, Loeb Classical Library (Cambridge, Mass.: Harvard University; London: William Heinemann, 1968), 2:195.

114. Sophocles, *Antigone,* trans. F. Storr, Loeb Classical Library (London: William Heinemann; New York: Macmillan, 1912), 1.353.

115. Bourne, *Argument,* 83.

116. The disintegration of the Roman *familia* has long been noted (and lamented) by modern classicists and scholars of antiquity. See Beryl Rowson, "The Roman Family," in *The Family in Ancient Rome,* ed. Beryl Rowson (Ithaca, N.Y.: Cornell University Press, 1986), 1-6.

117. Sotah 1:4, in Jacob Neusner, trans., *The Talmud of the Land of Israel: A Preliminary Translation and Explanation,* vol. 27, Sotah (Chicago: University of Chicago Press, 1984), 31-32.

118. Lucian, *Demonax,* trans. A. M. Harmon, Loeb Classical Library (New York: Macmillan, 1913), 149, 173.

119. Hans Dieter Betz, *Plutarch's Ethical Writings and Early Christian Literature,* Studia ad corpus hellenisticum Novi Testamenti 4 (Leiden: Brill, 1978), 233-34.

120. Plutarch, *Moralia,* vol. 6; trans. W. C. Helmbold, Loeb Classical Library (Cambridge, Mass.: Harvard University Press, 1939) 249.

121. Ibid., 255.

122. Ibid., 269.

123. Ibid., 253, 313, 315.

124. Ibid., 277.

125. Ibid., 275.

126. Ibid., 265, 267.

127. Ibid., 317.

128. Ibid., 255, 257.

129. "On Duties"; "On Fraternal Love," 4.27.20 = 4.660, 15–664, 18 Hense, in Abraham Malherbe, ed., *Moral Exhortation: A Greco-Roman Sourcebook* (Philadelphia: Westminster, 1986), 95.

130. Ibid.

131. "On Duties"; "On Fraternal Love," 4.27.20 = 4.660, 15–664, 18 Hense, in Malherbe, *Moral Exhortation,* 94.

132. Philostratus, *The Life of Apollonius of Tyana,* trans. F. C. Conybeare, vol. 1, Loeb Classical Library (New York: Macmillan, 1912), 31, 33, and 35.

133. Mitchell, "Envoys," 644.

134. Ibid., 645.

135. Ibid., 649.

136. Ibid., 650.

137. Clarice Martin, "The Rhetorical Function of Commercial Language in Paul's Letter to Philemon (Verse 18)," in Duane F. Watson, ed., *Persuasive Artistry: Studies in New Testament Rhetoric in Honor of George A. Kennedy,* Journal for the Study of the New Testament Supplement Series 50 (Sheffield: Sheffield Academic Press, 1991), 321–37.

138. Gary Wills, *Lincoln at Gettysburg* (New York: Simon and Schuster, 1992), 187.

139. In Langston Hughes and Arna Bontemps, eds., *The Book of Negro Folklore* (New York: Dodd, Mead, 1958), 605.

140. See Caroline Alexander, "Partners in the Slave Trade," *New York Times* Op-Ed, July 10, 1992, A29; Kenneth Noble, "An Influential Nigerian Insists West Owes Africa for Slavery," *New York Times International,* August 10, 1992, A2.

141. For an excellent review of efforts and arguments to secure African American reparations from Reconstruction to the present, see Lena Williams, "Group of Blacks Presses Case for Reparations for Slavery," *New York Times,* July 21, 1994. I am indebted to journalist Wallace V. Short for bringing this article to my attention. See also Eloise Salholz with Frank Washington, "Paying for the Sins of the Past," *Newsweek,* May 22, 1989, 44, which refers to the African American Summit as "a convention of black legislators in New Orleans."

142. David Ellen, "Payback Time," *New Republic* 201, no. 5 (July 31, 1989): 10.

143. Alexander, "Partners," A29.

144. Wills, *Lincoln at Gettysburg,* 168, n. 28.

145. "The Mistakes in the Gulf" *America* 159, no. 3 (July 23, 1988): 51.

146. Ibid.

147. *The Economist* 308, no. 7559 (July 16, 1988): 27.

148. Ibid.

149. R. Daniels, *Asian America: Chinese and Japanese in the United States since 1850* (Seattle: University of Washington Press, 1988) in Donna K. Nagata, "The Japanese-American Internment: Perceptions of Moral Community, Fairness, and Redress," *Journal of Social Issues* 46, no. 1 (Spring 1990): 138.

150. Nagata, "Internment," 140.

151. "In a sense we've come to our nation's capital to cash a check. When the architects of our republic wrote the magnificent words of the Constitution and the Declaration of Independence they were signing a promissory note to which every American was to fall heir. This note was the promise that all men, yes, black men as well as white men, would be guaranteed the unalienable rights of life, liberty, and the pursuit of happiness.

"It is obvious today that America has defaulted on this promissory note in so far as her citizens of color are concerned. Instead of honoring this sacred obligation, America has given the Negro people a bad check; a check which has come back marked 'insufficient funds'" (Martin Luther King Jr., "I Have a Dream," in Washington, *Testament,* 217).

152. Clarice Martin, "Rhetorical Function," 332–33.

153. See 2 Cor. 8:2; 1 Tim. 5:3–16; Ignatius, Smyrn 9.2. See the Th.D. dissertation by Judy Ravesloot Haley, "The Politics of Unity: Envoy and Audience in Ignatius' Letters to Smyrna," Harvard Divinity School, 1994. I have greatly benefited from consulting her treatment of benefaction and hospitality in the churches of Asia Minor with which Ignatius corresponded.

154. *Pace* Lightfoot, *Apostolic Fathers,* 2:35–36, who while recognizing the appearance of this verb in Ignatius's correspondence as a Pauline echo (see Magn 2.1;12.1; Rom. 5.2; Pol 1.1;6.2) did not consider it a pun on Onesimus' name.

155. Max E. Wilcox, *The Semitisms of Acts* (Oxford: Clarendon Press, 1965), 95.

156. Lightfoot, *Saint Paul's Epistles to the Colossians and Philemon,* 411.

157. Ernst Amling, "Eine Konjektur im Philemonbrief," *Zeitschrift für neutestamentliche Wissenschaft* 10 (1909): 261–62.

158. Jerome, *Vir. ill.* 8; see Gregory Dix, *Jew and Greek: A Study in the Primitive Church* (Westminster: Dacre, 1955), 75

159. The earliest manuscript witness is Codex Fuldensis from the sixth century: *Ad Philemonen. Philemoni familiares litteras facit pro Onesimo seruo eius. Scribit autem ei a Roma de carcere* ("To Philemon. He [i.e., Paul] wrote an intimate letter for his slave Onesimus. He wrote it while imprisoned in Rome"), in Donatien de Bruyne, "Prologues bibliques d'origine Marcionite." *Révue Bénédictine* 24 (1907): 15.

160. Henry Cadbury, *The Style and Literary Method of Luke* (Cambridge, Mass.: Harvard University, 1920; reprint: New York: Kraus, 1969).

161. On this see Theodor Zahn, *Introduction to the New Testament,* vol. 3, trans. John Moore Trout et al. (New York: Charles Scribner's Sons, 1917), 5, n. 4, where he cites Wettstein and Bengal as having made this identification.

162. The words of Martin Luther King, Jr., provide the moral for this story. From *Where Do We Go from Here: Chaos or Community?* (Boston: Beacon Press, 1968), 37.

Appendix: Subscriptions

163. Metzger, *Textual Commentary,* 658–59.

164. Lines 270–272, in Hanson, "Martyrdom," 338; English translation, 339.

Bibliography

Aeschines. *Embassy.* Trans. Charles Darwin Adams. Loeb Classical Library. London: Heinemann, 1919.

Alexander, Caroline. "Partners in the Slave Trade." *New York Times,* July 10, 1992, A29.

Allen, Richard. *Life Experiences and Gospel Labors.* Introduction by George A. Singleton. 1793; reprint: New York and Nashville: Abingdon, 1960.

Amling, Ernst. "Eine Konjektur im Philemonbrief." *Zeitschrift für neutestamentliche Wissenschaft* 10 (1909): 261–62.

Baur, Chrysostomus. *John Chrysostom and His Time.* Trans. Sr. M. Gonzaga. London: Sands, 1959.

Baur, Ferdinand Christian. *Paul the Apostle of Jesus Christ.* Trans. A. Menzies. 2 vols. Edinburgh: Williams and Norgate, 1873–75.

Bellet, P. "Analecta Coptica." *Catholic Bible Quarterly* 40 (1978): 37–52.

Betz, Hans Dieter. *Plutarch's Ethical Writings and Early Christian Literature.* Studia ad corpus hellenisticum Novi Testamenti 4. Leiden: Brill, 1978.

Bonnet, Maximilian, ed. *Acta Apostolorum Apocrypha.* Leipzig: Mendelssohn, 1903; reprint: Hildesheim, Zurich, and New York: Olms, 1990.

Bornkamm, Gunther. "Presbus ktl." *Theological Dictionary of the New Testament* 6 (1968): 651–83.

Bourne, George. *A Condensed Anti-Slavery Bible Argument.* New York: S. W. Benedict, 1845.

Branch, Taylor. *Parting the Waters.* New York: Simon and Schuster, 1988.

Brightman, William, ed. *The Orations of Saint Athanasius against the Arians.* London: Clarendon, 1873.

Briggs, Sheila. "Can an Enslaved God Liberate? Hermeneutical Reflections on Philippians 2:6–11." *Semeia* 47 (1989): 137–53.

Buckland, W. W. *The Roman Law of Slavery.* Cambridge: Cambridge University Press, 1908; reprint: New York: AMS Press, 1969.

Cadbury, Henry Joel. *The Style and Literary Method of Luke.* Cambridge, Mass.: Harvard University Press, 1920; reprint: New York: Kraus, 1969.

Callahan, Allen. "Paul's Epistle to Philemon: Toward an Alternative Argumentum." *Harvard Theological Review* 86, no. 4 (1993): 357–76.

———. "John Chrysostom on Philemon: A Response to Margaret M. Mitchell." *Harvard Theological Review* 88, no. 1 (1995): 149–56.

Callimachus. *Epigrams.* Trans. G. R. Mair. Loeb Classical Library. Cambridge: Harvard University Press, 1960.

Chase, Henry. *Chrysostom: A Study in the History of Biblical Interpretation.* Cambridge: Deighton Bell and Co.; London: George Bell and Sons, 1887.

Church, F. Forrester. "Rhetorical Structure and Design in Paul's Letter to Philemon." *Harvard Theological Review* 71 (1978): 17–33.

Clark, Elizabeth A. *Jerome, Chrysostom and Friends.* New York and Toronto: Edwin Mellen Press, 1979.

Corcoran, Gervase. "Slavery and the New Testament." *Milltown Studies* 1, no. 5 (1980): 1–40.

Daniels, R. *Asian America: Chinese and Japanese in the United States since 1850.* Seattle: University of Washington Press, 1988.

de Bruyne, Donatien. "Prologues bibliques d'origine Marcionite." *Revue Benedictine* 24 (1907): 1–16.

Deissmann, Adolph. *Light From the Ancient East.* Trans. Lionel Strachman. London, New York, and Toronto: Hodder & Stoughton, 1911.

Dix, Gregory. *Jew and Greek: A Study in the Primitive Church.* Westminster: Dacre, 1955.

Elkins, Stanley. *Slavery: A Problem in American Institutional and Economic Life.* Chicago: University of Chicago Press, 1959.

Ellen, David. "Payback Time." *New Republic* 201, no. 5 (July 31, 1989): 10.

Ellington, John. "La Bible Segond et la Nouvelle Version Segond Revisée." *Bible Translator* 31 (1980): 100–110.

Elliott, Neil. *Liberating Paul: The Justice of God and the Politics of the Apostle.* Maryknoll, N.Y.: Orbis, 1994.

Ellison, Ralph. *The Collected Essays of Ralph Ellison.* Ed. John Callahan. New York: Modern Library, 1995.

Fee, John Gregg. *An Anti-Slavery Manual.* Mayville, Ky., 1848; reprint: New York: Arno Press, 1969.

Finley, Moses. *Ancient Slavery and Modern Ideology.* London: Chatto and Windus, 1980.

Funk, Robert W. "The Apostolic Parousia: Form and Significance." In W. R. Farmer, C. F. D. Moule, and R. R. Niebuhr, eds., *Christian*

History and Interpretation. Cambridge: Cambridge University Press, 1974, 249–268.

Genovese, Eugene. "Rebelliousness and Docility in the Negro Slave: A Critique of the Elkins Thesis." *Civil War History* 13 (1966): 293–314; reprint in idem, *In Red and Black: Marxian Explorations in Southern and Afro-American History.* New York: Pantheon, 1971.

Haley, Judy Ravesloot. "The Politics of Unity: Envoy and Audience in Ignatius' Letters to Smyrna." Th.D. dissertation, Harvard Divinity School, 1994.

Hanson, Craig L. "A Greek Martyrdom Account of St. Onesimus." *Greek Orthodox Theological Review* 22, no. 3 (1977): 319–39.

Hennecke, Edgar, and Wilhelm Schneemelcher, eds. *New Testament Apocrypha.* Trans. A. J. B. Higgins et al. 2 vols. Philadelphia: Westminster, 1963–66.

Hock, Ronald F. "A Support for His Old Age: Paul's Plea on Behalf of Onesimus." In L. Michael White and O. Larry Yarbrough, eds., *The Social World of the First Christians: Essays in Honor of Wayne Meeks.* Minneapolis: Fortress, 1995, 67–81.

Horsley, G. H. R. *New Documents Illustrating Early Christianity.* Vol. 4: *A Review of the Greek Inscriptions and Papyri Published in 1977.* North Ryde, Australia: Ancient History Documentary Research Centre, Macquarie University, 1982.

Hughes, Langston, and Arna Bontemps, eds. *The Book of Negro Folklore.* New York: Dodd, Mead, 1958.

Johnstone, Henry, Jr. "Some Reflections on Argumentation." In idem, *Philosophy, Rhetoric and Argumentation.* University Park: Pennsylvania State University Press, 1965, 1–9.

King, Martin Luther, Jr. *Where Do We Go from Here: Chaos or Community?* Boston: Beacon Press, 1968.

———. "Letter from Birmingham Jail." In James Melvin Washington, ed., *A Testament of Hope.* San Francisco: Harper & Row, 1986, 289–302.

Knox, John. *Philemon among the Letters of Paul.* New York: Abingdon, 1935.

Kümmel, Werner Georg. *Introduction to the New Testament.* Trans. A. J. Mattill Jr. New York and Nashville: Abingdon, 1966.

Lampe, Peter. "Keine Sklavenflucht des Onesimus." *Zeitschrift für neutestamentliche Wissenschaft* 76 (1985): 135–37.

Lancashire, Douglas, et al. "The Bible in Modern Chinese: A Symposium." *Bible Translator* 11 (1960): 100–110.

Lee, G. M. "Eusebius on Saint Mark and the Beginnings of Christianity in Egypt." *Studia Patristica* 12 (1975): 422–31.

Lehmann, Richard. *Épître à Philemon: Le Christianisme primitif et l'esclavage.* Geneva: Labor et Fides, 1978.

Lightfoot, Joseph Barber. *Saint Paul's Epistles to the Colossians and Philemon.* London: Macmillan, 1875.

Lohmeyer, Ernst. *Die Brief an die Philipper, an die Kolosser und an Philemon.* Kritisch-exegetischer Kommentar über das Neue Testament 9. Göttingen: Vandenhoeck & Ruprecht, 1964.

Lohse, Eduard. *A Commentary on the Epistle to the Colossians and Philemon.* Ed. Helmut Koester. Trans. William Doehlman and Robert J. Karris. Philadelphia: Fortress, 1971.

Lucian. *Demonax.* Trans. A. M. Harmon. Loeb Classical Library. New York: Macmillan, 1913.

Luther, Martin. "Lecture on Philemon." In idem, *Luther's Works,* ed. Jaroslav Pelikan. St. Louis: Concordia Publishing House, 1955, 29. 95.

Malherbe, Abraham. *Social Aspects of Early Christianity.* 2nd ed. Philadelphia: Fortress, 1983.

————, ed. *Moral Exhortation: A Greco-Roman Sourcebook.* Philadelphia: Westminster, 1986.

Martin, Clarice. "The Rhetorical Function of Commercial Language in Paul's Letter to Philemon (Verse 18)." In Duane F. Watson, ed., *Persuasive Artistry: Studies in New Testament Rhetoric in Honor of George A. Kennedy.* Journal for the Study of the New Testament Supplement Series 50. Sheffield: Sheffield Academic Press, 1991, 321–37.

Metzger, Bruce. *A Textual Commentary on the Greek New Testament.* London and New York: United Bible Societies, 1971.

————, in Herbert G. May and Bruce Metzger, eds., *The Oxford Annotated Bible.* New York and Oxford: Oxford University Press, 1962, 1451.

"The Mistakes in the Gulf." *America* 1593 (July 23, 1988): 51.

Mitchell, Margaret M. "New Testament Envoys in the Context of Greco-Roman Diplomatic and Epistolary Conventions: The Example of Timothy and Titus." *Journal of Biblical Literature* 111 (1992): 641–62.

————. "John Chrysostom on Philemon: A Second Look." *Harvard Theological Review* 88, no. 1 (1995): 135–48.

Morrison, Larry. "The Religious Defense of American Slavery before 1830." *Journal of Religious Thought* 37, no. 2 (1980–81): 16–29.

Moule, C. F. D. *The Epistles of Paul the Apostle to the Colossians and Philemon.* Cambridge: Cambridge University Press, 1957.

Moule, Handley C. G. *Colossians and Philemon Studies: Lessons in Faith and Holiness.* London: Pickering and Inglis, 1930.

Nagata, Donna K. "The Japanese-American Internment: Perceptions of Moral Community, Fairness, and Redress." *Journal of Social Issues* 46 (1990): 133–46.

Neusner, Jacob, trans. *The Talmud of the Land of Israel: A Preliminary Translation and Explanation.* Vol. 27. *Sotah.* Chicago: University of Chicago Press, 1984.

Noble, Kenneth. "An Influential Nigerian Insists West Owes Africa for Slavery." *New York Times International.* August 10, 1992, A2.

Nordling, John G. "Onesimus Fugitivus: A Defense of the Runaway Slave Hypothesis in Philemon." *Journal for the Study of the New Testament* 41 (1991): 97–119.

Patterson, Orlando. *Slavery and Social Death.* Cambridge, Mass.: Harvard University Press, 1982.

Petersen, Norman. *Rediscovering Paul: Philemon and the Sociology of Paul's Narrative World.* Philadelphia: Fortress, 1985.

Philostratus. *The Life of Apollonius of Tyana.* Trans. F. C. Conybeare. Loeb Classical Library. New York: Macmillan, 1912.

Plutarch. *Moralia.* Vol. 6. Trans. W. C. Helmbold. Loeb Classical Library. Cambridge, Mass.: Harvard University Press, 1939.

Raboteau, Albert. *Slave Religion: The "Invisible Institution" in the Antebellum South.* Oxford: Oxford University Press, 1978.

Rawson, Beryl. "The Roman Family." In idem, *The Family in Ancient Rome.* Ithaca, N.Y.: Cornell University Press, 1986.

Salholz, Eloise and Frank Washington. "Paying for the Sins of the Past." *Newsweek,* May 22, 1989, 44.

Schaff, Phillip and Henry Wace, eds. *Nicene and Post-Nicene Fathers.* Second series. Reprint: Grand Rapids, Mich.: Eerdmans, 1978.

Scott, Walter, ed. and trans. *Hermetica.* 4 vols. Boston: Shambhala, 1985.

Shanks, Caroline L. "The Biblical Anti-Slavery Argument of the Decade 1830–1840." In Paul Finkelman, ed., *Religion and Slavery.* New York: Garland Publishing, 1989, 616–41.

Soards, Marion. "Some Neglected Theological Dimensions of Paul's Letter to Philemon." *Perspectives in Religious Studies* 17, no. 3 (1990): 209–19.

Sophocles. *Antigone.* Trans. F. Storr. Loeb Classical Library. London: Heinemann; New York: Macmillan, 1912.

Stuhlmacher, Peter. *Der Brief an Philemon.* Neukirchen-Vluyn: Neukirchener Verlag, 1981.

Theodore of Mopsuestia. *Theodori Episcopi Mopsuesteni in Beati Pauli Commentarii.* Cambridge: Cambridge University Press, 1880–82.

Vail, Stephen M. *The Bible Against Slavery.* (Concord, N.H.: Fogg, Hadley, 1864).

Vincent, Marvin R. *A Critical and Exegetical Commentary on the Epistles of the Philippians and to Philemon.* International Critical Commentary. Edinburgh: T. & T. Clark, 1897.

Wickert, Ulrich. "Der Philemonbrief — Privatbrief oder apostolisches Schreiben?" *Zeitschrift für neutestamentliche Wissenschaft* 52 (1961): 230–38.

Wilcox, Max E. *The Semitisms of Acts.* Oxford: Clarendon Press, 1965.

Williams, Lena. "Group of Blacks Presses Case for Reparations for Slavery." *New York Times,* July 21, 1994.

Wills, Garry. *Under God: Religion and American Politics.* New York: Simon and Schuster, 1990.

———. *Lincoln at Gettysburg.* New York: Simon and Schuster, 1992.

Winter, Sara. "Methodological Observations on a New Interpretation of Paul's Letter to Philemon." *Union Seminary Quarterly Review* 39 (1984): 203–12.

———. "Paul's Letter to Philemon." *New Testament Studies* 33 (1987): 1–15.

Xenophon. *Cyropaedia.* Trans. Walter Miller. Loeb Classical Library. Cambridge, Mass.: Harvard University Press; London: Heinemann, 1968.

Zahn, Theodor. *Introduction to the New Testament.* Trans. John Moore Trout. 3 vols. New York: Scribner's, 1917.

Index of Biblical Passages

Index of Names

Allen Dwight Callahan is assistant professor of New Testament at Harvard Divinity School.